55 Beef Recipes for Home

By: Kelly Johnson

Table of Contents

Classic Beef Dishes:

- Beef Stroganoff
- Beef Bourguignon
- Beef and Broccoli Stir-Fry
- Beef Wellington
- Beef Tacos
- Classic Meatloaf
- Beef Lasagna
- Chili Con Carne
- Beef Enchiladas
- Swiss Steak

Grilled and Barbecue Favorites:

- Grilled Steak with Chimichurri Sauce
- BBQ Beef Ribs
- Teriyaki Beef Skewers
- Korean Bulgogi
- Grilled Sirloin Steak
- Beef Kabobs with Vegetables
- Tandoori Beef
- Smoked Brisket
- Tex-Mex Fajitas
- Hawaiian Loco Moco

International Flavors:

- Thai Beef Salad
- Beef Rendang (Indonesian)
- Japanese Gyudon (Beef Bowl)
- Mexican Carne Asada
- Italian Beef Osso Buco
- Greek Moussaka
- Argentine Chimichurri Steak

- Brazilian Feijoada
- Vietnamese Shaking Beef (Bo Luc Lac)
- Chinese Hot and Sour Beef Soup

Quick and Easy Weeknight Dinners:

- Beef and Vegetable Stir-Fry
- One-Pot Beef and Mushroom Risotto
- Ground Beef Tacos
- Beef and Pepper Skillet
- Quick Beef Bolognese
- Beef and Noodle Stir-Fry
- Beef Quesadillas
- Mongolian Beef
- Beef and Vegetable Kabobs
- Beef and Black Bean Stir-Fry

Comfort Food Classics:

- Beef Pot Roast
- Beef and Potato Casserole
- Beef and Guinness Pie
- Stuffed Bell Peppers with Ground Beef
- Beef and Vegetable Stew
- Beef Shepherd's Pie
- Corned Beef and Cabbage
- Sloppy Joes
- Beef and Mushroom Pie
- Philly Cheesesteak Sandwich

Fusion and Creative Twists:

- Beef and Shrimp Spring Rolls
- Beef and Sweet Potato Curry
- Pineapple Beef Stir-Fry
- Beef and Blue Cheese Sliders
- Mediterranean Beef Skillet

Classic Beef Dishes:

Beef Stroganoff

Ingredients:

- 1.5 lbs (700g) beef sirloin or tenderloin, thinly sliced
- 2 tablespoons olive oil
- 1 onion, finely chopped
- 2 cloves garlic, minced
- 8 oz (225g) mushrooms, sliced
- 2 tablespoons butter
- 3 tablespoons all-purpose flour
- 1 cup (240ml) beef broth
- 2 tablespoons Dijon mustard
- 1 tablespoon Worcestershire sauce
- 1/2 cup (120ml) sour cream
- Salt and pepper to taste
- Fresh parsley, chopped, for garnish
- 12 oz (340g) egg noodles or rice, cooked (for serving)

Instructions:

> In a large skillet, heat the olive oil over medium-high heat. Add the thinly sliced beef and cook until browned on all sides. Remove the beef from the skillet and set aside.
>
> In the same skillet, add the butter and sauté the chopped onion until softened. Add the minced garlic and sliced mushrooms, cooking until the mushrooms release their moisture and become golden brown.
>
> Sprinkle the flour over the mushroom mixture and stir to combine. Cook for 1-2 minutes to eliminate the raw flour taste.
>
> Slowly add the beef broth to the skillet, stirring continuously to avoid lumps. Allow the mixture to simmer until it thickens.
>
> Stir in the Dijon mustard and Worcestershire sauce. Adjust the seasoning with salt and pepper to taste.
>
> Return the cooked beef to the skillet and simmer for an additional 5-7 minutes, allowing the flavors to meld.
>
> Reduce the heat to low, and stir in the sour cream until well combined. Be careful not to boil the mixture once the sour cream is added.

Serve the Beef Stroganoff over cooked egg noodles or rice. Garnish with chopped fresh parsley.

This Beef Stroganoff recipe is a comforting and rich dish with a creamy sauce that pairs perfectly with the tender beef. It's a timeless favorite that will surely be enjoyed by many.

Beef Bourguignon

Ingredients:

- 2.5 lbs (1.1 kg) beef chuck, cut into cubes
- Salt and black pepper to taste
- 3 tablespoons olive oil
- 1 large onion, finely chopped
- 3 cloves garlic, minced
- 3 carrots, peeled and sliced
- 2 cups (480 ml) red wine (Burgundy or any dry red wine)
- 2 cups (480 ml) beef broth
- 2 tablespoons tomato paste
- 1 bouquet garni (thyme, bay leaves, parsley)
- 1 lb (450g) small pearl onions, peeled
- 8 oz (225g) mushrooms, quartered
- 2 tablespoons all-purpose flour (optional, for thickening)
- Fresh parsley, chopped, for garnish

Instructions:

Preheat the oven to 325°F (163°C).
Season the beef cubes with salt and black pepper.
In a large oven-safe Dutch oven, heat olive oil over medium-high heat. Add the beef cubes in batches and brown on all sides. Remove and set aside.
In the same pot, add chopped onions, minced garlic, and sliced carrots. Sauté until the onions are translucent.
Pour in the red wine to deglaze the pot, scraping up any browned bits from the bottom.
Return the browned beef to the pot. Add beef broth, tomato paste, and the bouquet garni. Bring to a simmer.
Cover the pot and transfer it to the preheated oven. Cook for 2 to 2.5 hours or until the beef is tender.
In a separate pan, sauté the pearl onions and mushrooms in a bit of olive oil until they are golden brown.
If you prefer a thicker sauce, mix flour with a bit of water to create a smooth paste. Stir it into the beef stew during the last 15 minutes of cooking.
Add the sautéed pearl onions and mushrooms to the pot, stirring gently to combine. Adjust seasoning if needed.

Remove the bouquet garni, and discard it.
Serve the Beef Bourguignon over mashed potatoes, pasta, or crusty bread.
Garnish with chopped fresh parsley.

This Beef Bourguignon recipe delivers a rich, hearty stew with tender beef and a flavorful wine-infused broth. It's a classic French dish that's perfect for special occasions or when you want to treat yourself to a comforting and elegant meal.

Beef and Broccoli Stir-Fry

Ingredients:

- 1 lb (450g) flank steak, thinly sliced against the grain
- 3 cups broccoli florets
- 1/2 cup low-sodium soy sauce
- 3 tablespoons oyster sauce
- 2 tablespoons hoisin sauce
- 2 tablespoons rice vinegar
- 1 tablespoon sesame oil
- 2 tablespoons cornstarch
- 3 tablespoons vegetable oil, divided
- 3 cloves garlic, minced
- 1 teaspoon fresh ginger, grated
- 2 green onions, sliced (for garnish)
- Sesame seeds (optional, for garnish)
- Cooked white rice, for serving

Instructions:

In a bowl, mix together soy sauce, oyster sauce, hoisin sauce, rice vinegar, sesame oil, and cornstarch to create the marinade.

Place the thinly sliced flank steak in a shallow dish and pour half of the marinade over it. Allow it to marinate for at least 15-20 minutes.

In a wok or large skillet, heat 2 tablespoons of vegetable oil over medium-high heat.

Add the marinated beef to the hot wok, spreading it out to ensure even cooking. Stir-fry for 2-3 minutes or until the beef is browned and cooked through. Remove the beef from the wok and set it aside.

In the same wok, add the remaining tablespoon of vegetable oil. Stir in minced garlic and grated ginger, and sauté for about 1 minute until fragrant.

Add broccoli florets to the wok and stir-fry for 3-4 minutes until they are tender-crisp.

Return the cooked beef to the wok, along with the remaining marinade. Stir everything together and let it cook for an additional 2-3 minutes until the sauce thickens.

Garnish the Beef and Broccoli Stir-Fry with sliced green onions and sesame seeds, if desired.

Serve the stir-fry over cooked white rice.

This Beef and Broccoli Stir-Fry is a quick and flavorful dish that's perfect for busy weeknights. The combination of tender beef, crisp broccoli, and savory sauce makes it a crowd-pleaser.

Beef Wellington

Ingredients:

- 2.5 to 3 lbs (1.1 to 1.4 kg) beef tenderloin
- Salt and black pepper to taste
- 2 tablespoons olive oil
- 1 tablespoon Dijon mustard
- 1 pound (450g) mushrooms, finely chopped
- 4 tablespoons unsalted butter
- 2 cloves garlic, minced
- 1/2 cup (120ml) dry white wine
- 8 slices prosciutto or Parma ham
- 1 pound (450g) puff pastry, thawed if frozen
- 2 large eggs, beaten (for egg wash)
- Salt for seasoning the puff pastry

Instructions:

Preheat the oven to 400°F (200°C).
Season the beef tenderloin with salt and black pepper. Heat olive oil in a large skillet over high heat and sear the beef on all sides until browned. Remove from heat and let it cool. Brush the cooled beef with Dijon mustard.
In the same skillet, add butter and sauté the chopped mushrooms and garlic until the moisture is evaporated. Pour in the white wine and cook until the mixture becomes a dry paste. Let it cool.
Lay out the prosciutto or Parma ham slices on a sheet of plastic wrap, slightly overlapping. Spread the mushroom mixture over the ham.
Place the beef on top of the mushroom-covered ham and roll it tightly using the plastic wrap. Chill in the refrigerator for at least 15-20 minutes.
Roll out the puff pastry on a lightly floured surface. Unwrap the beef from the plastic wrap and place it in the center of the pastry. Fold the pastry over the beef, sealing the edges.
Brush the pastry with the beaten eggs for a golden finish. Sprinkle a little salt over the top.
Place the wrapped beef on a baking sheet and bake in the preheated oven for 25-30 minutes or until the pastry is golden brown.

Allow the Beef Wellington to rest for a few minutes before slicing. Serve the slices with your favorite sauce, such as a red wine reduction.

Beef Wellington is a show-stopping dish with layers of flavor and a beautiful presentation, making it ideal for special occasions or a luxurious dinner experience.

Beef Tacos

Ingredients:

For the Beef Filling:

- 1 lb ground beef
- 1 onion, finely chopped
- 2 cloves garlic, minced
- 1 tablespoon chili powder
- 1 teaspoon ground cumin
- 1/2 teaspoon paprika
- 1/2 teaspoon oregano
- Salt and black pepper to taste
- 1/2 cup beef broth
- 1 tablespoon tomato paste

For Assembling Tacos:

- Taco shells or tortillas
- Shredded lettuce
- Diced tomatoes
- Shredded cheese (cheddar or Mexican blend)
- Sour cream
- Salsa
- Fresh cilantro, chopped
- Lime wedges

Instructions:

Cook Beef Filling:
- In a skillet over medium heat, cook the ground beef until browned. Drain any excess fat.
- Add chopped onions and minced garlic to the skillet. Sauté until the onions are softened.

Season Beef:
- Stir in chili powder, ground cumin, paprika, oregano, salt, and black pepper. Cook for a couple of minutes until the spices are fragrant.

Add Liquid Ingredients:

- Pour in beef broth and add tomato paste. Stir well to combine. Simmer for 5-7 minutes until the mixture thickens.

Assemble Tacos:
- Warm the taco shells or tortillas according to the package instructions.
- Spoon the beef filling into each taco shell.

Add Toppings:
- Top the beef with shredded lettuce, diced tomatoes, shredded cheese, sour cream, salsa, and chopped fresh cilantro.

Serve:
- Serve the Beef Tacos with lime wedges on the side.

Feel free to customize your tacos with additional toppings like guacamole, jalapeños, or your favorite hot sauce. Enjoy your flavorful and satisfying Beef Tacos!

Classic Meatloaf

Ingredients:

For the Meatloaf:

- 1.5 lbs ground beef (or a mix of beef and pork)
- 1 cup breadcrumbs
- 1/2 cup milk
- 2 large eggs
- 1 onion, finely chopped
- 2 cloves garlic, minced
- 1/4 cup ketchup
- 2 tablespoons Worcestershire sauce
- 1 teaspoon dried thyme
- 1 teaspoon dried oregano
- Salt and black pepper to taste

For the Glaze:

- 1/2 cup ketchup
- 2 tablespoons brown sugar
- 1 tablespoon Dijon mustard

Instructions:

Preheat Oven:
- Preheat your oven to 350°F (175°C).

Prepare Meatloaf Mixture:
- In a large mixing bowl, combine ground beef, breadcrumbs, milk, eggs, chopped onion, minced garlic, ketchup, Worcestershire sauce, dried thyme, dried oregano, salt, and black pepper. Mix until well combined.

Shape the Meatloaf:
- Transfer the meat mixture to a greased baking dish or shape it into a loaf on a baking sheet.

Make Glaze:

- In a small bowl, whisk together ketchup, brown sugar, and Dijon mustard to make the glaze.

Apply Glaze:
- Brush or spread half of the glaze over the top of the meatloaf.

Bake:
- Bake in the preheated oven for about 50-60 minutes or until the internal temperature reaches 160°F (71°C).

Apply Remaining Glaze:
- In the last 10-15 minutes of baking, brush or spread the remaining glaze over the meatloaf.

Rest and Slice:
- Remove the meatloaf from the oven and let it rest for a few minutes before slicing.

Serve:
- Serve slices of the Classic Meatloaf with your favorite sides, such as mashed potatoes and green beans.

This Classic Meatloaf is a hearty and satisfying dish that's perfect for a comforting family dinner. Enjoy!

Beef Lasagna

Ingredients:

For the Bolognese Sauce:

- 1.5 lbs (680g) ground beef
- 1 onion, finely chopped
- 3 cloves garlic, minced
- 1 carrot, grated
- 1 celery stalk, finely chopped
- 1 can (28 oz / 800g) crushed tomatoes
- 2 tablespoons tomato paste
- 1 cup (240ml) beef broth
- 1/2 cup (120ml) red wine (optional)
- 2 teaspoons dried oregano
- 2 teaspoons dried basil
- Salt and black pepper to taste
- 2 tablespoons olive oil

For the Lasagna Layers:

- 9 lasagna noodles, cooked according to package instructions
- 3 cups (720g) ricotta cheese
- 2 large eggs
- 3 cups (300g) shredded mozzarella cheese
- 1 cup (100g) grated Parmesan cheese
- Fresh basil or parsley for garnish

Instructions:

Preheat the oven to 375°F (190°C).
In a large skillet, heat olive oil over medium heat. Add chopped onions, minced garlic, grated carrot, and chopped celery. Sauté until vegetables are softened. Add ground beef to the skillet, breaking it apart with a spatula. Cook until browned.
Stir in crushed tomatoes, tomato paste, beef broth, red wine (if using), dried oregano, dried basil, salt, and black pepper. Simmer for 20-30 minutes, allowing the flavors to meld.

In a separate bowl, combine ricotta cheese and eggs. Mix well.

Cook lasagna noodles according to package instructions. Drain and set aside.

In a greased 9x13-inch baking dish, spread a thin layer of the Bolognese sauce.

Place three lasagna noodles on top of the sauce, followed by a layer of the ricotta mixture, mozzarella cheese, and Bolognese sauce. Repeat these layers until you run out of ingredients, finishing with a layer of Bolognese sauce on top.

Sprinkle grated Parmesan cheese evenly over the top layer.

Cover the baking dish with aluminum foil and bake in the preheated oven for 25-30 minutes.

Remove the foil and bake for an additional 10-15 minutes or until the top is golden and bubbly.

Let the lasagna rest for 15 minutes before slicing.

Garnish with fresh basil or parsley before serving.

Beef Lasagna is a classic comfort food dish that's perfect for family dinners or special occasions. The layers of rich Bolognese sauce, creamy ricotta, and melted cheese create a satisfying and indulgent meal.

Chili Con Carne

Ingredients:

- 1.5 lbs (680g) ground beef
- 1 large onion, finely chopped
- 3 cloves garlic, minced
- 1 red bell pepper, chopped
- 1 can (15 oz / 425g) kidney beans, drained and rinsed
- 1 can (15 oz / 425g) black beans, drained and rinsed
- 1 can (14 oz / 400g) diced tomatoes
- 1 can (6 oz / 170g) tomato paste
- 2 cups (480ml) beef broth
- 1 cup (240ml) water
- 2 tablespoons chili powder
- 1 teaspoon ground cumin
- 1 teaspoon paprika
- 1/2 teaspoon cayenne pepper (adjust to taste)
- Salt and black pepper to taste
- 2 tablespoons olive oil
- Optional toppings: shredded cheddar cheese, sour cream, chopped green onions, fresh cilantro

Instructions:

In a large pot or Dutch oven, heat olive oil over medium heat. Add chopped onions and minced garlic, sautéing until they become translucent.
Add ground beef to the pot, breaking it apart with a spatula. Cook until browned.
Stir in chili powder, ground cumin, paprika, cayenne pepper, salt, and black pepper. Cook for an additional 2-3 minutes to toast the spices.
Add chopped red bell pepper and cook for another 2-3 minutes.
Pour in diced tomatoes, tomato paste, kidney beans, black beans, beef broth, and water. Stir to combine.
Bring the mixture to a boil, then reduce the heat to low. Cover and simmer for at least 30 minutes, stirring occasionally.
Taste and adjust the seasoning, adding more salt or spices if needed.
Continue to simmer uncovered for an additional 15-20 minutes to allow the flavors to meld and the chili to thicken.
Serve the Chili Con Carne hot, ladled into bowls.

Top with shredded cheddar cheese, a dollop of sour cream, chopped green onions, and fresh cilantro if desired.

Chili Con Carne is a hearty and flavorful dish that's perfect for warming up on chilly days. Adjust the spice level to your liking and enjoy this classic comfort food with your favorite toppings.

Beef Enchiladas

Ingredients:

For the Enchilada Sauce:

- 2 tablespoons vegetable oil
- 2 tablespoons all-purpose flour
- 4 tablespoons chili powder
- 1 teaspoon ground cumin
- 1/2 teaspoon garlic powder
- 1/4 teaspoon dried oregano
- 2 cups (480ml) chicken or beef broth
- 1 can (14 oz / 400g) crushed tomatoes
- Salt and black pepper to taste

For the Filling:

- 1.5 lbs (680g) ground beef
- 1 onion, finely chopped
- 2 cloves garlic, minced
- 1 can (15 oz / 425g) black beans, drained and rinsed
- 1 cup (240ml) corn kernels (fresh or frozen)
- 1 teaspoon ground cumin
- 1 teaspoon chili powder
- Salt and black pepper to taste
- 2 cups (200g) shredded cheddar cheese

For Assembly:

- 10-12 large flour tortillas
- Additional shredded cheese for topping
- Fresh cilantro, chopped, for garnish
- Sour cream, for serving

Instructions:

Prepare the Enchilada Sauce:
- In a medium saucepan, heat vegetable oil over medium heat. Stir in flour and cook for 1-2 minutes to make a roux.
- Add chili powder, ground cumin, garlic powder, and dried oregano. Cook for an additional 1-2 minutes.
- Gradually whisk in the broth and crushed tomatoes until smooth.
- Bring the mixture to a simmer and cook for 10-15 minutes, stirring occasionally. Season with salt and black pepper to taste.

Prepare the Filling:
- In a skillet, brown the ground beef over medium heat. Drain excess fat.
- Add chopped onions and minced garlic, cooking until onions are softened.
- Stir in black beans, corn, ground cumin, chili powder, salt, and black pepper. Cook for an additional 5 minutes.
- Remove from heat and stir in 1 cup of shredded cheddar cheese.

Assemble the Beef Enchiladas:
- Preheat the oven to 375°F (190°C).
- Spoon a small amount of enchilada sauce into the bottom of a baking dish.
- Place a portion of the beef filling in the center of each tortilla, roll them up, and place them seam side down in the baking dish.
- Pour the remaining enchilada sauce over the rolled tortillas, spreading it evenly.
- Sprinkle additional shredded cheese over the top.
- Bake in the preheated oven for 20-25 minutes or until the cheese is melted and bubbly.

Serve:
- Garnish with chopped fresh cilantro.
- Serve the Beef Enchiladas hot, with a dollop of sour cream on the side.

These Beef Enchiladas are a delicious and comforting meal, perfect for a family dinner or entertaining guests. Customize the filling and toppings to suit your preferences for a flavorful and satisfying experience.

Swiss Steak

Ingredients:

- 2 lbs (900g) beef round steak, about 1/2 inch thick, trimmed of excess fat
- 1 cup (120g) all-purpose flour
- Salt and black pepper to taste
- 2 tablespoons vegetable oil
- 1 large onion, thinly sliced
- 2 carrots, sliced into rounds
- 2 celery stalks, chopped
- 2 cloves garlic, minced
- 1 can (14 oz / 400g) crushed tomatoes
- 1 cup (240ml) beef broth
- 1 teaspoon dried thyme
- 1 teaspoon dried oregano
- 1 teaspoon paprika
- 1 bay leaf
- Chopped fresh parsley for garnish

Instructions:

Preheat the oven to 325°F (163°C).
Trim excess fat from the round steak and cut it into serving-size pieces. Season the steak pieces with salt and black pepper.
Dredge the steak pieces in flour, shaking off any excess.
In a large oven-safe Dutch oven or skillet, heat vegetable oil over medium-high heat. Brown the steak pieces on both sides. Work in batches to avoid overcrowding the pan. Remove browned steak pieces and set them aside.
In the same pot, add sliced onions, carrots, and chopped celery. Sauté until the vegetables are softened.
Stir in minced garlic and cook for an additional minute until fragrant.
Add crushed tomatoes, beef broth, dried thyme, dried oregano, paprika, and the bay leaf to the pot. Stir to combine.
Return the browned steak pieces to the pot, nestling them into the tomato and vegetable mixture.
Cover the pot with a lid and transfer it to the preheated oven. Bake for 1.5 to 2 hours or until the meat is tender and cooked through.

Remove the bay leaf before serving. Adjust the seasoning with salt and pepper if needed.
Serve the Swiss Steak over mashed potatoes, rice, or noodles.
Garnish with chopped fresh parsley before serving.

Swiss Steak is a comforting and hearty dish, with tender beef and a rich tomato-based sauce. It's a classic recipe that makes for a satisfying meal, especially when served with your favorite side.

Grilled and Barbecue Favorites:

Grilled Steak with Chimichurri Sauce

Ingredients:

For the Steak:

- 2 lbs (900g) sirloin or ribeye steaks (about 1-inch thick)
- Salt and black pepper to taste
- 2 tablespoons olive oil
- 2 cloves garlic, minced
- 1 teaspoon smoked paprika (optional)

For the Chimichurri Sauce:

- 1 cup fresh parsley, chopped
- 1/2 cup fresh cilantro, chopped
- 3 cloves garlic, minced
- 1/4 cup red wine vinegar
- 1/2 cup extra virgin olive oil
- 1 teaspoon dried oregano
- 1/2 teaspoon red pepper flakes (adjust to taste)
- Salt and black pepper to taste

Instructions:

    Prepare the Chimichurri Sauce:
- In a bowl, combine chopped parsley, cilantro, minced garlic, red wine vinegar, extra virgin olive oil, dried oregano, red pepper flakes, salt, and black pepper.
- Mix well and let it sit at room temperature for at least 15-20 minutes to allow the flavors to meld.

    Prepare the Grilled Steak:
- Preheat the grill to medium-high heat.
- Season the steaks with salt, black pepper, and smoked paprika (if using). Drizzle with olive oil and rub minced garlic over the steaks.
- Grill the steaks for about 4-5 minutes per side for medium-rare, adjusting the time based on your desired doneness.

- Remove the steaks from the grill and let them rest for a few minutes before slicing.

Serve:
- Slice the grilled steaks against the grain into thin strips.
- Drizzle the chimichurri sauce over the sliced steak or serve it on the side for dipping.
- Garnish with additional fresh herbs if desired.

Enjoy:
- Serve the Grilled Steak with Chimichurri Sauce alongside your favorite sides like roasted vegetables, potatoes, or a fresh green salad.

This Grilled Steak with Chimichurri Sauce is a flavorful and vibrant dish, combining the rich taste of perfectly grilled steak with the zesty and herby notes of the chimichurri sauce. It's a wonderful choice for a delicious and impressive meal.

BBQ Beef Ribs

Ingredients:

For the Beef Ribs:

- 3-4 lbs (1.4-1.8 kg) beef back ribs
- Salt and black pepper to taste
- 2 tablespoons smoked paprika
- 1 tablespoon garlic powder
- 1 tablespoon onion powder
- 1 teaspoon cayenne pepper (adjust to taste)
- 1 tablespoon brown sugar (optional)

For the BBQ Sauce:

- 1 cup (240 ml) ketchup
- 1/2 cup (120 ml) apple cider vinegar
- 1/4 cup (60 ml) Worcestershire sauce
- 1/4 cup (60 ml) soy sauce
- 1/4 cup (60 ml) brown sugar
- 2 teaspoons Dijon mustard
- 2 teaspoons smoked paprika
- 1 teaspoon garlic powder
- Salt and black pepper to taste

Instructions:

Prepare the Beef Ribs:
- Preheat your grill or smoker to 225-250°F (107-121°C).
- Remove the membrane from the back of the ribs for better flavor penetration.
- In a small bowl, mix together salt, black pepper, smoked paprika, garlic powder, onion powder, cayenne pepper, and brown sugar.
- Rub the spice mixture evenly over the beef ribs, covering them on all sides.

Smoke/Grill the Ribs:

- Place the seasoned beef ribs on the preheated grill or smoker, bone side down.
- Maintain a consistent temperature and smoke the ribs for 4-5 hours, or until the meat is tender and has a nice bark.

Prepare the BBQ Sauce:
- In a saucepan over medium heat, combine ketchup, apple cider vinegar, Worcestershire sauce, soy sauce, brown sugar, Dijon mustard, smoked paprika, garlic powder, salt, and black pepper.
- Simmer the sauce for about 15-20 minutes, stirring occasionally, until it thickens slightly.

Glaze the Ribs:
- During the last 30 minutes of cooking, brush the beef ribs with the prepared BBQ sauce.
- Repeat the brushing every 10 minutes or so, building up a flavorful glaze on the ribs.

Serve:
- Once the ribs are done, let them rest for a few minutes.
- Slice the ribs between the bones, and serve with extra BBQ sauce on the side.

Enjoy:
- Serve the BBQ Beef Ribs with your favorite side dishes, such as coleslaw, baked beans, or cornbread.

These BBQ Beef Ribs are a delicious and smoky treat, perfect for a backyard barbecue or a special weekend meal. The combination of the savory rub and the sweet and tangy BBQ sauce creates a mouthwatering flavor that will impress your guests or satisfy your family's cravings.

Teriyaki Beef Skewers

Ingredients:

For the Teriyaki Marinade:

- 1.5 lbs (680g) beef sirloin or flank steak, thinly sliced
- 1/2 cup (120ml) soy sauce
- 1/4 cup (60ml) mirin
- 2 tablespoons sake (or white wine)
- 3 tablespoons brown sugar
- 2 cloves garlic, minced
- 1 teaspoon fresh ginger, grated
- 2 tablespoons sesame oil
- 1 tablespoon cornstarch (optional, for thickening)

For Skewers:

- Wooden or metal skewers
- Vegetables of your choice (bell peppers, onions, cherry tomatoes)
- Sesame seeds for garnish (optional)
- Green onions, sliced, for garnish (optional)

Instructions:

Prepare the Teriyaki Marinade:
- In a bowl, whisk together soy sauce, mirin, sake, brown sugar, minced garlic, grated ginger, and sesame oil. This is your teriyaki marinade.

Marinate the Beef:
- Place the thinly sliced beef in a shallow dish or a zip-top bag. Pour half of the teriyaki marinade over the beef, reserving the other half for later. Make sure the beef is well-coated. Marinate for at least 30 minutes to 1 hour in the refrigerator.

Prepare the Skewers:
- If you're using wooden skewers, soak them in water for about 30 minutes to prevent them from burning on the grill.

- Thread the marinated beef slices onto the skewers, alternating with your chosen vegetables.

Grill or Cook:
- Preheat the grill or grill pan to medium-high heat.
- Grill the skewers for about 2-3 minutes per side or until the beef is cooked to your liking and has a nice char.

Prepare Glaze:
- While grilling, heat the reserved teriyaki marinade in a small saucepan. If you'd like a thicker glaze, mix in cornstarch dissolved in a little water and simmer until it thickens.

Glaze and Garnish:
- Brush the cooked skewers with the heated teriyaki glaze.
- Garnish with sesame seeds and sliced green onions if desired.

Serve:
- Serve the Teriyaki Beef Skewers over a bed of steamed rice or alongside your favorite side dishes.

These Teriyaki Beef Skewers are a delicious combination of savory, sweet, and umami flavors. They make for a fantastic appetizer, main course, or even a delightful addition to a summer barbecue. Enjoy!

Korean Bulgogi

Ingredients:

- 1.5 lbs (680g) thinly sliced beef (ribeye or sirloin)
- 1 pear, grated
- 1 onion, finely chopped
- 3 cloves garlic, minced
- 1/4 cup soy sauce
- 2 tablespoons brown sugar
- 1 tablespoon honey
- 1 tablespoon sesame oil
- 1 tablespoon mirin (rice wine)
- 1 teaspoon grated fresh ginger
- 1 tablespoon sesame seeds (for garnish)
- 2 green onions, sliced (for garnish)

Instructions:

Prepare Marinade:
- In a bowl, combine grated pear, chopped onion, minced garlic, soy sauce, brown sugar, honey, sesame oil, mirin, and grated ginger. This is your bulgogi marinade.

Marinate the Beef:
- Place the thinly sliced beef in a shallow dish or a zip-top bag. Pour the bulgogi marinade over the beef, ensuring it is well-coated. Marinate for at least 30 minutes to 2 hours in the refrigerator. For a more intense flavor, you can marinate it overnight.

Cook Bulgogi:
- Heat a grill or grill pan over medium-high heat.
- Remove the beef from the marinade, allowing any excess to drip off.
- Grill the marinated beef slices for 2-3 minutes per side or until cooked to your liking.

Garnish:
- Sprinkle sesame seeds and sliced green onions over the cooked bulgogi.

Serve:

- Serve the Korean Bulgogi over steamed rice or wrapped in lettuce leaves. It can also be accompanied by a side of kimchi and other Korean banchan (side dishes).

Tips:

- For a tenderizing effect, the pear in the marinade helps break down the proteins in the meat.
- Bulgogi can also be cooked in a pan on the stove if a grill is not available.

Korean Bulgogi is a delightful and flavorful dish with a perfect balance of sweet and savory notes. Enjoy the rich taste of marinated beef with the distinctive Korean flair!

Grilled Sirloin Steak

Ingredients:

- 4 sirloin steaks (about 8 oz / 225g each)
- 2 tablespoons olive oil
- 2 cloves garlic, minced
- 1 teaspoon dried rosemary
- 1 teaspoon dried thyme
- Salt and black pepper to taste
- Optional: Steak seasoning or rub of your choice

Instructions:

Prepare the Steaks:
- Take the sirloin steaks out of the refrigerator at least 30 minutes before grilling to bring them to room temperature. This helps them cook more evenly.

Marinate the Steaks:
- In a bowl, mix together olive oil, minced garlic, dried rosemary, dried thyme, salt, and black pepper. If desired, you can also use a steak seasoning or rub of your choice.
- Rub the mixture over the sirloin steaks, ensuring they are evenly coated. Allow them to marinate for at least 15-20 minutes.

Preheat the Grill:
- Preheat your grill to medium-high heat. Make sure the grates are clean and well-oiled to prevent sticking.

Grill the Sirloin Steaks:
- Place the marinated sirloin steaks on the preheated grill.
- Grill for about 4-5 minutes per side for medium-rare, adjusting the time based on your desired doneness. You can use a meat thermometer to check for doneness (145°F / 63°C for medium-rare, 160°F / 71°C for medium, 170°F / 77°C for well-done).

Rest the Steaks:
- Once the steaks reach your preferred level of doneness, remove them from the grill and let them rest for about 5 minutes. This allows the juices to redistribute throughout the meat.

Serve:

- Slice the grilled sirloin steaks against the grain into thin strips.
- Serve the steak slices on a platter or individual plates. You can accompany them with your favorite sides, such as grilled vegetables, mashed potatoes, or a fresh salad.

Optional: Baste with Extra Marinade:
- If desired, you can baste the steaks with any remaining marinade during the last few minutes of grilling for an extra burst of flavor.

Grilled Sirloin Steak is a simple yet delicious dish that showcases the natural flavors of the beef with the added touch of aromatic herbs and garlic. Enjoy the succulence of perfectly grilled steaks at your next barbecue or dinner gathering.

Beef Kabobs with Vegetables

Ingredients:

For the Marinade:

- 1.5 lbs (680g) beef sirloin or top sirloin, cut into 1-inch cubes
- 1/4 cup olive oil
- 1/4 cup soy sauce
- 2 tablespoons balsamic vinegar
- 2 tablespoons Worcestershire sauce
- 2 cloves garlic, minced
- 1 teaspoon Dijon mustard
- 1 teaspoon dried thyme
- 1 teaspoon dried rosemary
- Salt and black pepper to taste

For the Kabobs:

- Cherry tomatoes
- Bell peppers, cut into chunks (use a variety of colors)
- Red onion, cut into wedges
- Mushrooms, cleaned and halved
- Zucchini, sliced into rounds

Instructions:

Prepare the Marinade:
- In a bowl, whisk together olive oil, soy sauce, balsamic vinegar, Worcestershire sauce, minced garlic, Dijon mustard, dried thyme, dried rosemary, salt, and black pepper.

Marinate the Beef:
- Place the beef cubes in a large, shallow dish or a zip-top bag. Pour half of the marinade over the beef, reserving the other half for later. Ensure the beef is well-coated. Marinate for at least 30 minutes to 2 hours in the refrigerator.

Prepare the Skewers:

- If using wooden skewers, soak them in water for about 30 minutes to prevent them from burning on the grill.
- Preheat the grill to medium-high heat.
- Thread the marinated beef cubes onto the skewers, alternating with cherry tomatoes, bell peppers, red onion wedges, mushrooms, and zucchini slices.

Grill the Kabobs:
- Place the assembled beef kabobs on the preheated grill.
- Grill for about 10-15 minutes, turning occasionally, or until the beef reaches your desired level of doneness and the vegetables are tender.

Baste with Reserved Marinade:
- During the last few minutes of grilling, baste the kabobs with the reserved marinade for added flavor.

Serve:
- Remove the beef kabobs from the grill and let them rest for a few minutes.
- Serve the kabobs on a platter, and you can sprinkle them with additional fresh herbs or a drizzle of balsamic glaze if desired.

Enjoy these Beef Kabobs with Vegetables for a delicious and colorful meal that's perfect for grilling season. They make a fantastic addition to any barbecue or outdoor gathering.

Smoked Brisket

Ingredients:

For the Brisket:

- 1 whole brisket, approximately 10-12 lbs (4.5-5.4 kg)
- 1/4 cup kosher salt
- 1/4 cup black pepper, coarsely ground
- 1/4 cup paprika
- 2 tablespoons brown sugar
- 1 tablespoon garlic powder
- 1 tablespoon onion powder
- 1 tablespoon chili powder
- 1 teaspoon cayenne pepper (adjust to taste)
- Wood chunks or chips for smoking (hickory, oak, or mesquite are popular choices)

For the Mop Sauce (optional):

- 1 cup beef broth
- 1/2 cup apple cider vinegar
- 1/4 cup Worcestershire sauce
- 1/4 cup vegetable oil
- 1 tablespoon hot sauce
- 1 tablespoon kosher salt
- 1 tablespoon black pepper

Instructions:

Prepare the Brisket:
- Trim excess fat from the brisket, leaving about 1/4 inch. Pat the brisket dry with paper towels.

Create the Rub:
- In a bowl, mix together kosher salt, black pepper, paprika, brown sugar, garlic powder, onion powder, chili powder, and cayenne pepper to create the rub.

Apply the Rub:

- Generously coat the entire brisket with the rub, ensuring all sides are well-covered. Pat the rub into the meat.

Let it Rest:
- Place the brisket on a baking sheet and let it rest at room temperature for about 1 hour. This allows the rub to penetrate the meat.

Prepare the Smoker:
- Preheat your smoker to a temperature of 225-250°F (107-121°C). Use hardwood chunks or chips for smoking.

Smoke the Brisket:
- Place the brisket on the smoker, fat side up, and insert a meat thermometer into the thickest part of the meat.
- Smoke the brisket until it reaches an internal temperature of around 195-203°F (91-95°C). This process can take 10-12 hours, depending on the size of the brisket.

Optional Mop Sauce:
- Combine all the ingredients for the mop sauce in a bowl. Baste the brisket every 1-2 hours during the smoking process.

Rest and Slice:
- Once the brisket reaches the desired temperature, remove it from the smoker, wrap it in foil, and let it rest for at least 1 hour. This allows the juices to redistribute.
- Slice the brisket against the grain into 1/4 to 1/2-inch slices.

Serve:
- Serve the smoked brisket slices on a platter. You can enjoy it as is or with your favorite barbecue sauce.

Smoked brisket is a classic barbecue dish that requires time and patience, but the results are well worth it. The combination of the flavorful rub and slow smoking process creates tender and delicious meat that's perfect for any barbecue or special occasion.

Tex-Mex Fajitas

Ingredients:

For the Marinade:

- 1.5 lbs (680g) skirt steak or flank steak, thinly sliced
- 1/4 cup olive oil
- 1/4 cup lime juice
- 3 cloves garlic, minced
- 1 teaspoon ground cumin
- 1 teaspoon chili powder
- 1 teaspoon smoked paprika
- 1 teaspoon dried oregano
- Salt and black pepper to taste

For the Fajitas:

- 1 large onion, thinly sliced
- 2 bell peppers (assorted colors), thinly sliced
- Flour or corn tortillas
- Fresh cilantro, chopped (for garnish)
- Sour cream (for serving)
- Guacamole or sliced avocados (for serving)
- Salsa (for serving)
- Lime wedges (for serving)

Instructions:

Prepare the Marinade:
- In a bowl, whisk together olive oil, lime juice, minced garlic, ground cumin, chili powder, smoked paprika, dried oregano, salt, and black pepper.

Marinate the Steak:
- Place the thinly sliced steak in a shallow dish or a zip-top bag. Pour the marinade over the steak, ensuring it is well-coated. Marinate for at least 30 minutes to 2 hours in the refrigerator.

Cook the Fajitas:
- Heat a large skillet or grill pan over medium-high heat.

- Add the marinated steak slices and cook for 2-3 minutes per side or until cooked to your liking. Remove the steak from the skillet and set it aside.
- In the same skillet, add sliced onions and bell peppers. Sauté for about 5-7 minutes or until they are tender-crisp.

Warm the Tortillas:
- While the vegetables are cooking, warm the tortillas in a dry skillet or on the grill for about 20 seconds per side. Stack them and keep them warm in a clean kitchen towel.

Assemble the Fajitas:
- Place a portion of the cooked steak, sautéed vegetables, and any desired toppings onto each tortilla.
- Garnish with chopped cilantro and serve with sides like sour cream, guacamole, salsa, and lime wedges.

Serve:
- Serve Tex-Mex Fajitas immediately and enjoy!

Tex-Mex Fajitas are a quick and flavorful dish that's perfect for a casual weeknight dinner or a festive gathering. Customize your fajitas with your favorite toppings and enjoy the delicious combination of tender steak, sautéed vegetables, and zesty flavors.

Hawaiian Loco Moco

Ingredients:

For the Rice:

- 4 cups cooked white rice

For the Hamburger Patties:

- 1.5 lbs (680g) ground beef
- Salt and black pepper to taste
- 1 tablespoon Worcestershire sauce
- 1 tablespoon soy sauce
- 1 clove garlic, minced
- 1/2 cup breadcrumbs
- 1 large egg

For the Gravy:

- 2 tablespoons unsalted butter
- 1/4 cup all-purpose flour
- 3 cups beef or chicken broth
- 2 tablespoons soy sauce
- Salt and black pepper to taste

For the Eggs:

- 4 large eggs

For Garnish:

- Green onions, chopped
- Sesame seeds (optional)

Instructions:

Prepare the Rice:
- Cook the white rice according to package instructions and set aside.

Make the Hamburger Patties:
- In a bowl, combine ground beef, salt, black pepper, Worcestershire sauce, soy sauce, minced garlic, breadcrumbs, and egg. Mix until well combined.
- Shape the mixture into 4 hamburger patties.

Cook the Hamburger Patties:
- Heat a skillet or grill pan over medium-high heat. Cook the hamburger patties for about 4-5 minutes per side, or until they reach your desired level of doneness.

Prepare the Gravy:
- In the same skillet, melt butter over medium heat. Add flour and whisk continuously to form a roux.
- Gradually whisk in the beef or chicken broth to avoid lumps. Add soy sauce, salt, and black pepper. Continue to whisk until the gravy thickens. Reduce heat and simmer for a few minutes.

Cook the Eggs:
- In a separate pan, fry or poach the eggs according to your preference.

Assemble the Loco Moco:
- Place a serving of cooked rice on a plate.
- Top the rice with a hamburger patty.
- Pour a generous amount of gravy over the hamburger patty and rice.
- Add a fried or poached egg on top.

Garnish and Serve:
- Garnish with chopped green onions and sesame seeds (if using).
- Serve the Hawaiian Loco Moco hot and enjoy the flavorful combination of rice, hamburger patty, egg, and savory gravy!

Hawaiian Loco Moco is a comfort food classic that originated in Hawaii and has become a beloved dish with its unique blend of flavors. Enjoy this hearty and satisfying meal that captures the essence of Hawaiian cuisine.

International Flavors:

Thai Beef Salad

Ingredients:

For the Beef:

- 1 lb (450g) beef sirloin or flank steak
- 2 tablespoons soy sauce
- 1 tablespoon fish sauce
- 1 tablespoon oyster sauce
- 1 tablespoon vegetable oil
- 1 teaspoon sugar
- 2 cloves garlic, minced
- 1 teaspoon grated ginger
- Lime wedges for serving

For the Salad:

- Mixed salad greens (lettuce, cucumber, cherry tomatoes, etc.)
- 1 red onion, thinly sliced
- 1 bell pepper, thinly sliced
- Fresh cilantro leaves, chopped
- Fresh mint leaves, chopped
- Roasted peanuts, crushed

For the Dressing:

- 3 tablespoons lime juice
- 2 tablespoons fish sauce
- 1 tablespoon soy sauce
- 1 tablespoon brown sugar
- 1 tablespoon sesame oil
- 1 red chili, finely chopped (adjust to taste)

Instructions:

Marinate and Cook the Beef:

- In a bowl, mix together soy sauce, fish sauce, oyster sauce, vegetable oil, sugar, minced garlic, and grated ginger.
- Place the beef in a shallow dish and pour half of the marinade over it. Let it marinate for about 30 minutes.
- Heat a grill or grill pan over medium-high heat. Grill the beef for 3-4 minutes per side or until it reaches your desired doneness. Let it rest for a few minutes, then slice it thinly.

Prepare the Dressing:
- In a small bowl, whisk together lime juice, fish sauce, soy sauce, brown sugar, sesame oil, and chopped red chili. Adjust the seasoning to your taste.

Assemble the Salad:
- In a large bowl, combine mixed salad greens, thinly sliced red onion, sliced bell pepper, cilantro leaves, and mint leaves.
- Add the sliced grilled beef on top.
- Drizzle the dressing over the salad and toss gently to combine.

Serve:
- Transfer the Thai Beef Salad to a serving platter or individual plates.
- Sprinkle crushed roasted peanuts on top.
- Serve immediately, garnished with extra fresh herbs and lime wedges on the side.

Enjoy the vibrant and flavorful Thai Beef Salad as a light and refreshing meal that combines the richness of grilled beef with the zesty and aromatic Thai dressing.

Beef Rendang (Indonesian)

Ingredients:

For the Spice Paste (Rempah):

- 6 shallots, peeled
- 4 cloves garlic, peeled
- 2 inches (5 cm) ginger, peeled
- 2 inches (5 cm) galangal, peeled
- 2 lemongrass stalks, white part only, sliced
- 5 red chillies, seeded (adjust to taste)
- 5 dried red chillies, soaked in hot water
- 1 tablespoon ground coriander
- 1 tablespoon ground cumin
- 1 teaspoon turmeric powder

For the Beef:

- 2 lbs (900g) beef stew meat, cut into cubes
- 2 cans (27 oz / 800ml) coconut milk
- 3 kaffir lime leaves
- 2 turmeric leaves (optional)
- 2 stalks lemongrass, bruised
- 1 tablespoon tamarind paste
- 2 tablespoons palm sugar or brown sugar
- Salt to taste

Instructions:

Prepare the Spice Paste (Rempah):
- In a blender or food processor, combine all the spice paste ingredients. Blend into a smooth paste.

Cook the Beef:
- In a large pot or wok, heat a bit of oil over medium heat. Add the spice paste and sauté until fragrant.
- Add the beef cubes and cook until browned.

- Pour in the coconut milk, kaffir lime leaves, turmeric leaves (if using), and bruised lemongrass stalks. Stir well.
- Add tamarind paste, palm sugar (or brown sugar), and salt to taste. Mix thoroughly.

Simmering:
- Bring the mixture to a boil, then reduce the heat to low. Let it simmer uncovered for about 2-3 hours, stirring occasionally, until the beef becomes tender, the sauce thickens, and the coconut milk reduces.
- Keep an eye on it towards the end to prevent burning. Adjust the seasoning as needed.

Finish Cooking:
- Continue simmering until the rendang turns dark brown and the oil separates from the mixture. This is a sign that the rendang is ready.

Serve:
- Remove the kaffir lime leaves, turmeric leaves, and lemongrass stalks.
- Serve the Beef Rendang with steamed rice or traditional Indonesian rice cakes called "ketupat."

Enjoy the rich and flavorful Indonesian Beef Rendang, a dish known for its tender, slow-cooked beef and aromatic spice blend. This dish is often served during special occasions and celebrations.

Japanese Gyudon (Beef Bowl)

Ingredients:

- 1 lb (450g) thinly sliced beef (such as ribeye or sirloin)
- 1 large onion, thinly sliced
- 2 green onions, sliced (white and green parts separated)
- 3 tablespoons soy sauce
- 2 tablespoons mirin
- 2 tablespoons sake (or dry white wine)
- 1 tablespoon sugar
- 1 tablespoon vegetable oil
- 1 teaspoon grated fresh ginger
- 1 1/2 cups dashi stock or beef broth
- Steamed rice for serving
- Pickled red ginger (beni shoga) for garnish (optional)
- Nori (dried seaweed) strips for garnish (optional)
- Shichimi togarashi (Japanese seven spice) for extra spice (optional)

Instructions:

Prepare the Sauce:
- In a bowl, whisk together soy sauce, mirin, sake, and sugar until the sugar is dissolved. Set aside.

Cook the Beef and Onions:
- Heat vegetable oil in a large skillet or pan over medium heat. Add the sliced onions and cook until they become translucent.
- Add the thinly sliced beef to the pan and cook until it's no longer pink.
- Stir in grated ginger and the white parts of the sliced green onions.

Add the Sauce:
- Pour the prepared sauce over the beef and onions. Mix well to ensure even coating.

Add Dashi Stock or Beef Broth:
- Pour in the dashi stock or beef broth and bring the mixture to a simmer. Let it simmer for a few minutes to allow the flavors to meld.

Simmer Until Onions Are Soft:
- Continue simmering until the onions are soft and the beef is cooked through. This usually takes about 5-7 minutes.

Serve Over Rice:

- Serve the Gyudon over steamed rice in bowls.

Garnish and Serve:
- Garnish with the green parts of the sliced green onions, pickled red ginger (beni shoga), nori strips, and a sprinkle of shichimi togarashi if desired.

Enjoy:
- Gyudon is best enjoyed hot and can be served with a side of miso soup or a simple Japanese salad.

Japanese Gyudon is a delicious and comforting dish that is quick to make and full of savory flavors. It's a popular choice for a quick and satisfying meal in Japanese cuisine.

Mexican Carne Asada

Ingredients:

For the Marinade:

- 2 lbs (900g) flank or skirt steak
- Juice of 3 limes
- Juice of 1 orange
- 4 cloves garlic, minced
- 1/4 cup chopped fresh cilantro
- 1/4 cup olive oil
- 1 teaspoon ground cumin
- 1 teaspoon chili powder
- 1 teaspoon dried oregano
- Salt and black pepper to taste

For Serving:

- Corn or flour tortillas
- Salsa or pico de gallo
- Guacamole
- Sour cream
- Fresh cilantro, chopped
- Lime wedges

Instructions:

Prepare the Marinade:
- In a bowl, whisk together lime juice, orange juice, minced garlic, chopped cilantro, olive oil, ground cumin, chili powder, dried oregano, salt, and black pepper.

Marinate the Steak:
- Place the flank or skirt steak in a shallow dish or a zip-top bag. Pour the marinade over the steak, making sure it is well-coated. Marinate for at least 30 minutes to 2 hours in the refrigerator.

Preheat the Grill:
- Preheat your grill or grill pan to medium-high heat.

Grill the Carne Asada:

- Remove the steak from the marinade and let any excess drip off.
- Grill the steak for about 4-6 minutes per side, depending on your desired level of doneness. Flank steak is best when cooked to medium-rare or medium.

Rest and Slice:
- Once cooked, let the carne asada rest for a few minutes before slicing. Slice the steak thinly against the grain.

Warm the Tortillas:
- Heat the tortillas on the grill for about 20 seconds on each side or until warm.

Serve:
- Serve the sliced carne asada on warm tortillas.
- Top with salsa or pico de gallo, guacamole, sour cream, and fresh cilantro.
- Squeeze lime wedges over the top for an extra burst of flavor.

Enjoy:
- Enjoy the Mexican Carne Asada as tacos, burritos, or on its own with your favorite side dishes.

Mexican Carne Asada is a delicious and versatile dish, perfect for grilling and enjoying in various Mexican-inspired meals. The flavorful marinade gives the steak a zesty and savory taste that pairs wonderfully with your favorite toppings and accompaniments.

Italian Beef Osso Buco

Ingredients:

- 4 beef shanks, about 2 inches thick
- Salt and black pepper to taste
- All-purpose flour for dredging
- 1/4 cup olive oil
- 1 onion, finely chopped
- 2 carrots, peeled and finely chopped
- 2 celery stalks, finely chopped
- 4 cloves garlic, minced
- 1 cup dry white wine
- 1 can (28 oz) crushed tomatoes
- 1 cup beef broth
- 1 teaspoon dried oregano
- 1 teaspoon dried thyme
- 2 bay leaves
- Zest of 1 lemon
- 1/4 cup fresh parsley, chopped (for garnish)

Gremolata (Optional):

- Zest of 1 lemon
- 2 tablespoons fresh parsley, chopped
- 1 clove garlic, minced

Instructions:

Preheat the Oven:
- Preheat the oven to 350°F (175°C).

Prepare the Beef Shanks:
- Season the beef shanks with salt and black pepper. Dredge each shank in flour, shaking off excess.

Brown the Beef Shanks:
- In a large ovenproof pot or Dutch oven, heat olive oil over medium-high heat. Brown the beef shanks on all sides until golden brown. This may take about 5-7 minutes per side. Remove the shanks and set them aside.

Sauté the Vegetables:

- In the same pot, add chopped onion, carrots, celery, and minced garlic. Sauté until the vegetables are softened.

Deglaze with Wine:
- Pour in the dry white wine, scraping the bottom of the pot to release any flavorful bits. Allow the wine to simmer for a few minutes.

Add Tomatoes and Broth:
- Stir in crushed tomatoes, beef broth, dried oregano, dried thyme, bay leaves, and lemon zest. Bring the mixture to a simmer.

Return Beef Shanks:
- Return the browned beef shanks to the pot, ensuring they are partially submerged in the liquid.

Braise in the Oven:
- Cover the pot and transfer it to the preheated oven. Braise for about 2 to 2.5 hours or until the beef is tender and falling off the bone.

Prepare Gremolata (Optional):
- In a small bowl, mix together lemon zest, chopped parsley, and minced garlic to create the gremolata.

Serve:
- Remove the bay leaves from the pot. Serve the Osso Buco over a bed of creamy polenta, mashed potatoes, or risotto.
- Garnish with chopped fresh parsley and, if desired, a sprinkle of gremolata.

Enjoy:
- Enjoy this classic Italian Beef Osso Buco with its rich and flavorful sauce!

Beef Osso Buco is a hearty and comforting dish that captures the essence of Italian cuisine. The slow braising process results in tender and succulent meat, complemented by a luscious tomato-based sauce. Serve it with your favorite side for a satisfying meal.

Greek Moussaka

Ingredients:

For the Eggplant Layer:

- 2 large eggplants, thinly sliced
- Salt for sprinkling
- Olive oil for brushing

For the Meat Sauce:

- 1 lb (450g) ground lamb or beef
- 1 large onion, finely chopped
- 3 cloves garlic, minced
- 1 can (14 oz / 400g) crushed tomatoes
- 2 tablespoons tomato paste
- 1 teaspoon dried oregano
- 1 teaspoon dried thyme
- 1 teaspoon ground cinnamon
- Salt and black pepper to taste

For the Bechamel Sauce:

- 1/2 cup (115g) unsalted butter
- 1/2 cup (60g) all-purpose flour
- 4 cups (960ml) whole milk, warmed
- 1/2 teaspoon ground nutmeg
- Salt and black pepper to taste
- 2 large eggs, beaten
- 1 cup (100g) grated Parmesan cheese

Instructions:

Preheat the Oven:
- Preheat your oven to 375°F (190°C).

Prepare the Eggplants:

- Place the thinly sliced eggplants on a baking sheet and sprinkle with salt. Let them sit for about 30 minutes to release excess moisture. Pat them dry with paper towels.
- Brush the eggplant slices with olive oil and roast them in the oven until they are golden brown and tender. Set aside.

Make the Meat Sauce:
- In a large skillet, cook the ground lamb or beef over medium heat until browned. Drain excess fat.
- Add chopped onions and minced garlic to the skillet. Cook until the onions are softened.
- Stir in crushed tomatoes, tomato paste, dried oregano, dried thyme, ground cinnamon, salt, and black pepper. Simmer the mixture for about 15-20 minutes until it thickens.

Prepare the Bechamel Sauce:
- In a saucepan, melt butter over medium heat. Stir in flour and cook for a few minutes until it forms a paste.
- Gradually whisk in the warmed milk, nutmeg, salt, and black pepper. Continue whisking until the sauce thickens.
- Remove the saucepan from heat and let it cool slightly. Whisk in beaten eggs and grated Parmesan cheese.

Assemble the Moussaka:
- In a greased baking dish, layer half of the roasted eggplant slices.
- Spread the meat sauce over the eggplant layer.
- Add the remaining eggplant slices on top.
- Pour the bechamel sauce over the top, ensuring it covers the entire surface.

Bake in the Oven:
- Bake the moussaka in the preheated oven for about 45-50 minutes or until the top is golden brown and the dish is set.

Rest and Serve:
- Allow the moussaka to rest for 15-20 minutes before slicing.
- Serve the moussaka warm, and enjoy this classic Greek dish!

Greek Moussaka is a delicious and hearty casserole made with layers of eggplant, flavorful meat sauce, and a creamy bechamel topping. It's a comforting dish that showcases the rich flavors of Mediterranean cuisine.

Argentine Chimichurri Steak

Ingredients:

For the Chimichurri Sauce:

- 1 cup fresh parsley, finely chopped
- 4 cloves garlic, minced
- 2 tablespoons fresh oregano, finely chopped
- 1 teaspoon red pepper flakes (adjust to taste)
- 1/4 cup red wine vinegar
- 1/2 cup extra-virgin olive oil
- Salt and black pepper to taste

For the Steak:

- 4 beef steaks (ribeye or sirloin), about 8 oz (225g) each
- Salt and black pepper to taste
- Olive oil for brushing

Instructions:

Prepare the Chimichurri Sauce:
- In a bowl, combine finely chopped fresh parsley, minced garlic, chopped fresh oregano, red pepper flakes, red wine vinegar, and extra-virgin olive oil.
- Mix well until all the ingredients are combined. Season with salt and black pepper to taste.
- Let the chimichurri sauce sit for at least 15-20 minutes to allow the flavors to meld. You can also prepare it in advance and refrigerate for more intense flavors.

Prepare the Steaks:
- Season the steaks with salt and black pepper on both sides.
- Brush the steaks with olive oil to help the seasoning adhere and prevent sticking on the grill.

Grill the Steaks:
- Preheat the grill to medium-high heat.

- Grill the steaks for about 4-5 minutes per side for medium-rare, adjusting the time based on your desired level of doneness.
- You can also use a meat thermometer to check for doneness (145°F / 63°C for medium-rare, 160°F / 71°C for medium, 170°F / 77°C for well-done).

Rest the Steaks:
- Once the steaks reach your preferred level of doneness, remove them from the grill and let them rest for about 5 minutes. This allows the juices to redistribute throughout the meat.

Serve:
- Slice the grilled steaks against the grain into thin strips.
- Drizzle the chimichurri sauce generously over the sliced steaks.
- Serve the Argentine Chimichurri Steak with your favorite side dishes, such as grilled vegetables, potatoes, or a fresh salad.

Argentine Chimichurri Steak is a classic and flavorful dish that showcases the vibrant and herbaceous taste of chimichurri sauce. The combination of a perfectly grilled steak and the zesty chimichurri creates a delightful culinary experience. Enjoy it as a main course for a delicious and satisfying meal.

Brazilian Feijoada

Ingredients:

For the Feijoada:

- 1 lb (450g) black beans, dried
- 1 lb (450g) pork shoulder, cubed
- 1/2 lb (225g) smoked sausage or linguica, sliced
- 1/2 lb (225g) chorizo sausage, sliced
- 1/2 lb (225g) bacon, chopped
- 1 large onion, finely chopped
- 4 cloves garlic, minced
- 2 bay leaves
- 1 orange, sliced (for garnish)
- Salt and black pepper to taste

For the Rice:

- 2 cups white rice
- 4 cups water
- Salt to taste

For the Farofa (Optional):

- 1 cup cassava flour (farinha de mandioca)
- 2 tablespoons butter
- Salt to taste

For the Orange Vinaigrette:

- 1 orange, juiced
- 2 tablespoons white wine vinegar
- 1/4 cup olive oil
- Salt and black pepper to taste

Instructions:

Prepare the Beans:
- Rinse the black beans and soak them overnight in cold water. Drain and rinse the beans before cooking.
- In a large pot, cover the soaked beans with water and bring to a boil. Reduce the heat to low, cover, and simmer until the beans are tender (about 1-1.5 hours).

Cook the Meats:
- In a separate pan, cook the pork shoulder, smoked sausage, chorizo, and chopped bacon until browned.
- Add the cooked meats to the pot of black beans.

Saute Onions and Garlic:
- In the same pan used for the meats, sauté finely chopped onions and minced garlic until softened.
- Add the sautéed onions and garlic to the pot of beans and meats.

Simmer with Bay Leaves:
- Add bay leaves to the pot, season with salt and black pepper, and simmer the feijoada for another 30-45 minutes until the flavors meld.

Prepare the Rice:
- Rinse the rice under cold water until the water runs clear.
- In a separate pot, combine rice, water, and salt. Bring to a boil, then reduce heat to low, cover, and simmer until the rice is cooked and water is absorbed (about 15-20 minutes).

Make the Farofa (Optional):
- In a skillet, melt butter and add cassava flour. Stir continuously until the flour is toasted and golden brown. Season with salt.

Prepare the Orange Vinaigrette:
- In a bowl, whisk together orange juice, white wine vinegar, olive oil, salt, and black pepper to create the vinaigrette.

Serve:
- Serve the feijoada over rice, garnished with orange slices.
- Optional: Serve farofa on the side and drizzle the orange vinaigrette over the feijoada.

Brazilian Feijoada is a hearty and flavorful stew that combines beans and a variety of meats. It's a traditional dish often served during festive occasions. Enjoy it with rice, farofa, and a refreshing orange vinaigrette for a true Brazilian culinary experience.

Vietnamese Shaking Beef (Bo Luc Lac)

Ingredients:

For the Marinade:

- 1.5 lbs (680g) beef tenderloin or sirloin, cut into bite-sized cubes
- 3 cloves garlic, minced
- 2 tablespoons oyster sauce
- 2 tablespoons soy sauce
- 1 tablespoon fish sauce
- 1 tablespoon sugar
- 1 teaspoon black pepper
- 2 tablespoons vegetable oil

For the Vinaigrette Dipping Sauce:

- 2 tablespoons rice vinegar
- 1 tablespoon soy sauce
- 1 tablespoon sugar
- 1/4 cup water
- 1 clove garlic, minced
- 1 Thai bird chili, minced (optional)

For Serving:

- Mixed salad greens (lettuce, watercress, or arugula)
- Sliced tomatoes
- Sliced red onions
- Lime wedges

Instructions:

   Marinate the Beef:
   - In a bowl, combine minced garlic, oyster sauce, soy sauce, fish sauce, sugar, black pepper, and vegetable oil to create the marinade.

- Add the beef cubes to the marinade and coat them evenly. Allow the beef to marinate for at least 30 minutes to an hour in the refrigerator.

Prepare the Vinaigrette Dipping Sauce:
- In a small bowl, whisk together rice vinegar, soy sauce, sugar, water, minced garlic, and minced Thai bird chili (if using). Set aside.

Cook the Beef:
- Heat a large skillet or wok over high heat. Add a bit of oil to the pan.
- Once the pan is very hot, add the marinated beef cubes. Cook in batches to avoid overcrowding the pan. Allow the beef to sear without stirring for about 1-2 minutes to achieve a nice crust.
- Toss or shake the pan to turn the beef cubes and sear on all sides. Cook until the beef is cooked to your desired level of doneness, which is usually medium-rare to medium.

Assemble the Salad:
- In a large bowl, toss the cooked beef with mixed salad greens, sliced tomatoes, and sliced red onions.

Serve:
- Arrange the salad on a serving platter or individual plates.
- Drizzle the vinaigrette dipping sauce over the beef and salad.
- Serve the Vietnamese Shaking Beef with lime wedges on the side.

Enjoy:
- Enjoy this flavorful and vibrant Vietnamese dish, Bo Luc Lac, with its tender and well-seasoned beef served over a bed of fresh salad greens!

Vietnamese Shaking Beef, or Bo Luc Lac, is a delicious and visually appealing dish that combines tender marinated beef with a zesty vinaigrette dipping sauce. It's often served with a refreshing salad, creating a delightful balance of flavors and textures.

Chinese Hot and Sour Beef Soup

Ingredients:

For the Broth:

- 6 cups beef broth
- 2 tablespoons soy sauce
- 2 tablespoons rice vinegar
- 1 tablespoon dark soy sauce
- 1 tablespoon hoisin sauce
- 1 tablespoon sesame oil
- 1 teaspoon sugar
- 1/2 teaspoon white pepper
- 1/2 teaspoon crushed red pepper flakes (adjust to taste)

For the Soup:

- 1/2 lb (225g) beef sirloin or flank, thinly sliced
- 1 cup shiitake mushrooms, sliced
- 1/2 cup bamboo shoots, thinly sliced
- 1/2 cup firm tofu, diced
- 1/4 cup wood ear mushrooms, rehydrated and thinly sliced
- 1/4 cup dried lily buds, rehydrated
- 2 eggs, beaten
- 1/4 cup cornstarch mixed with 1/4 cup water (slurry)
- Green onions, chopped (for garnish)
- Fresh cilantro, chopped (for garnish)
- White pepper and soy sauce (to taste)

Instructions:

Prepare the Broth:
- In a large pot, combine beef broth, soy sauce, rice vinegar, dark soy sauce, hoisin sauce, sesame oil, sugar, white pepper, and crushed red pepper flakes. Bring the mixture to a gentle simmer.

Add Ingredients to the Broth:

- Add the thinly sliced beef, shiitake mushrooms, bamboo shoots, tofu, wood ear mushrooms, and rehydrated lily buds to the simmering broth. Cook for about 5-7 minutes until the beef is cooked through.

Thicken the Soup:
- Pour in the cornstarch slurry while stirring the soup continuously. Allow the soup to thicken to your desired consistency.

Add Beaten Eggs:
- While stirring the soup, slowly pour in the beaten eggs in a thin stream. The eggs will cook and create silky strands in the soup.

Adjust Seasoning:
- Taste the soup and adjust the seasoning with white pepper and soy sauce as needed. Add more vinegar or sugar to achieve the desired balance of sour and sweet flavors.

Serve:
- Ladle the hot and sour beef soup into bowls.
- Garnish with chopped green onions and fresh cilantro.
- Serve the Chinese Hot and Sour Beef Soup hot and enjoy!

This soup is known for its bold and contrasting flavors, featuring the heat from white pepper and the tanginess from vinegar. The combination of tender beef, mushrooms, tofu, and other ingredients makes it a hearty and satisfying dish, perfect for warming up on a chilly day.

Quick and Easy Weeknight Dinners:

Beef and Vegetable Stir-Fry

Ingredients:

For the Marinade:

- 1 lb (450g) beef sirloin or flank, thinly sliced
- 2 tablespoons soy sauce
- 1 tablespoon oyster sauce
- 1 tablespoon hoisin sauce
- 1 tablespoon cornstarch
- 1 teaspoon sesame oil
- 1 teaspoon sugar
- 1/2 teaspoon black pepper

For the Stir-Fry:

- 2 tablespoons vegetable oil (for cooking)
- 3 cups mixed vegetables (broccoli, bell peppers, snap peas, carrots, etc.), sliced
- 3 cloves garlic, minced
- 1 tablespoon fresh ginger, grated
- 2 tablespoons soy sauce
- 1 tablespoon oyster sauce
- 1 tablespoon hoisin sauce
- 1 tablespoon cornstarch mixed with 2 tablespoons water (slurry)
- Green onions, chopped (for garnish)
- Sesame seeds (for garnish, optional)
- Cooked rice or noodles for serving

Instructions:

Marinate the Beef:
- In a bowl, combine sliced beef with soy sauce, oyster sauce, hoisin sauce, cornstarch, sesame oil, sugar, and black pepper. Allow it to marinate for at least 15-20 minutes.

Prepare the Vegetables:

- Slice the mixed vegetables into bite-sized pieces. Ensure that they are uniform in size for even cooking.

Cook the Beef:
- Heat vegetable oil in a wok or large skillet over high heat.
- Add the marinated beef slices and stir-fry for 2-3 minutes until they are browned and cooked through. Remove the beef from the wok and set it aside.

Stir-Fry the Vegetables:
- In the same wok, add a bit more oil if needed. Stir-fry the minced garlic and grated ginger for about 30 seconds until aromatic.
- Add the sliced vegetables to the wok and stir-fry for 3-4 minutes until they are crisp-tender.

Combine Beef and Vegetables:
- Return the cooked beef to the wok with the vegetables. Mix everything together.

Prepare the Sauce:
- In a small bowl, whisk together soy sauce, oyster sauce, hoisin sauce, and the cornstarch slurry.
- Pour the sauce over the beef and vegetables. Stir continuously until the sauce thickens and coats the ingredients.

Garnish and Serve:
- Garnish the beef and vegetable stir-fry with chopped green onions and sesame seeds if desired.
- Serve the stir-fry over cooked rice or noodles.

Enjoy:
- Enjoy this delicious and quick Beef and Vegetable Stir-Fry as a flavorful and nutritious meal!

This versatile stir-fry recipe allows you to use a variety of vegetables, making it a colorful and nutritious dish. The savory and slightly sweet sauce enhances the flavors of the beef and vegetables, creating a tasty and satisfying meal.

One-Pot Beef and Mushroom Risotto

Ingredients:

- 1 lb (450g) beef sirloin or tenderloin, thinly sliced
- 1 cup Arborio rice
- 8 oz (225g) mushrooms, sliced
- 1 onion, finely chopped
- 3 cloves garlic, minced
- 4 cups beef broth, kept warm
- 1 cup dry red wine
- 1/2 cup grated Parmesan cheese
- 2 tablespoons butter
- 2 tablespoons olive oil
- 1 teaspoon dried thyme
- Salt and black pepper to taste
- Chopped fresh parsley for garnish

Instructions:

Prep Ingredients:
- Season the beef slices with salt and black pepper. Set aside.
- In a separate bowl, combine Arborio rice with a bit of salt and set it aside.

Sear the Beef:
- In a large, deep skillet or a wide saucepan, heat olive oil over medium-high heat. Add the sliced beef and sear for 1-2 minutes per side until browned. Remove the beef from the skillet and set it aside.

Sauté Mushrooms and Aromatics:
- In the same skillet, add a bit more olive oil if needed. Sauté the chopped onion and minced garlic until softened.
- Add sliced mushrooms and cook until they release their moisture and become golden brown.

Toast the Rice:
- Add Arborio rice to the skillet and cook for 1-2 minutes until it is lightly toasted, stirring frequently.

Deglaze with Wine:
- Pour in the dry red wine and stir, scraping the bottom of the skillet to release any flavorful bits. Allow the wine to reduce by half.

Add Thyme and Broth:
- Sprinkle dried thyme over the rice mixture. Begin adding the warm beef broth, one ladle at a time, stirring constantly and allowing the liquid to be absorbed before adding more.
- Continue this process until the rice is cooked to al dente texture. This usually takes about 18-20 minutes.

Finish the Risotto:
- Once the rice is cooked, stir in the seared beef slices.
- Add grated Parmesan cheese and butter. Stir until the cheese is melted, and the risotto becomes creamy.

Adjust Seasoning and Garnish:
- Taste the risotto and adjust the seasoning with salt and black pepper if needed.
- Garnish with chopped fresh parsley.

Serve:
- Serve the One-Pot Beef and Mushroom Risotto immediately, and enjoy this comforting and flavorful dish!

This one-pot recipe combines the rich flavors of beef and mushrooms with creamy risotto, creating a comforting and satisfying meal. The method allows for a deliciously creamy texture without constant stirring, making it an excellent option for a cozy dinner.

Ground Beef Tacos

Ingredients:

For the Taco Filling:

- 1 lb (450g) ground beef
- 1 small onion, finely diced
- 2 cloves garlic, minced
- 1 packet taco seasoning mix (or use homemade seasoning)
- 1/2 cup water
- Salt and pepper to taste

For Serving:

- Taco shells (soft or hard)
- Shredded lettuce
- Diced tomatoes
- Shredded cheese (cheddar or Mexican blend)
- Sour cream
- Salsa
- Jalapeño slices (optional)
- Chopped cilantro (optional)
- Lime wedges

Instructions:

Cook the Ground Beef:
- In a skillet over medium-high heat, cook the ground beef until browned, breaking it apart with a spoon as it cooks.

Add Onion and Garlic:
- Add finely diced onion and minced garlic to the skillet. Cook for a few minutes until the onion is softened.

Season the Beef:
- Sprinkle the taco seasoning mix over the beef and stir to combine. If using homemade seasoning, add it along with salt and pepper to taste.

Add Water:
- Pour in the water and mix well. Allow the mixture to simmer for 5-7 minutes or until the liquid is mostly absorbed, and the flavors meld.

Prepare Taco Shells:
- While the beef is cooking, warm the taco shells according to the package instructions.

Assemble Tacos:
- Spoon the seasoned ground beef mixture into the taco shells.
- Top with shredded lettuce, diced tomatoes, shredded cheese, sour cream, salsa, jalapeño slices, chopped cilantro, and a squeeze of lime juice.

Serve:
- Arrange the assembled ground beef tacos on a serving platter.
- Serve immediately, allowing everyone to customize their tacos with their favorite toppings.

Enjoy:
- Enjoy these delicious and customizable Ground Beef Tacos for a quick and satisfying meal!

Ground Beef Tacos are a classic and versatile dish that is quick to make and perfect for a family dinner or casual gathering. The seasoned beef pairs wonderfully with a variety of fresh toppings, allowing everyone to create their perfect taco.

Beef and Pepper Skillet

Ingredients:

- 1 lb (450g) beef sirloin or flank, thinly sliced
- 2 tablespoons vegetable oil
- 1 onion, thinly sliced
- 1 red bell pepper, thinly sliced
- 1 yellow bell pepper, thinly sliced
- 1 green bell pepper, thinly sliced
- 3 cloves garlic, minced
- 2 tablespoons soy sauce
- 1 tablespoon oyster sauce
- 1 tablespoon hoisin sauce
- 1 teaspoon sugar
- 1 teaspoon cornstarch
- 1/2 teaspoon black pepper
- Green onions, sliced (for garnish)
- Cooked rice or noodles (for serving)

Instructions:

Prepare the Beef:
- In a bowl, combine thinly sliced beef with soy sauce, oyster sauce, hoisin sauce, sugar, cornstarch, and black pepper. Allow it to marinate for at least 15-20 minutes.

Cook the Beef:
- Heat vegetable oil in a large skillet or wok over high heat.
- Add the marinated beef slices and stir-fry for 2-3 minutes until they are browned and cooked through. Remove the beef from the skillet and set it aside.

Saute Onions and Peppers:
- In the same skillet, add a bit more oil if needed. Stir-fry thinly sliced onions until they are softened.
- Add thinly sliced red, yellow, and green bell peppers to the skillet. Continue to stir-fry for 3-4 minutes until the peppers are crisp-tender.

Combine Beef and Peppers:

- Return the cooked beef to the skillet with the sautéed peppers and onions. Mix everything together.

Adjust Seasoning:
- Taste the mixture and adjust the seasoning if needed. You can add more soy sauce or black pepper according to your preference.

Serve:
- Serve the Beef and Pepper Skillet over cooked rice or noodles.
- Garnish with sliced green onions.

Enjoy:
- Enjoy this quick and flavorful Beef and Pepper Skillet for a delicious and satisfying meal!

This Beef and Pepper Skillet is a simple yet tasty dish that combines tender slices of beef with colorful bell peppers. The savory and slightly sweet sauce enhances the flavors, making it a great option for a quick weeknight dinner. Serve it over rice or noodles for a complete and satisfying meal.

Quick Beef Bolognese

Ingredients:

- 1 lb (450g) ground beef
- 2 tablespoons olive oil
- 1 onion, finely chopped
- 2 carrots, finely chopped
- 2 celery stalks, finely chopped
- 3 cloves garlic, minced
- 1 teaspoon dried oregano
- 1 teaspoon dried basil
- 1/2 teaspoon red pepper flakes (optional)
- 1 can (28 oz / 800g) crushed tomatoes
- 1/2 cup red wine (optional)
- Salt and black pepper to taste
- 1/4 cup fresh parsley, chopped (for garnish)
- Grated Parmesan cheese (for serving)
- Cooked pasta (spaghetti, fettuccine, or your choice)

Instructions:

Cook the Ground Beef:
- In a large skillet or saucepan, heat olive oil over medium-high heat. Add ground beef and cook until browned, breaking it apart with a spoon as it cooks.

Saute Vegetables:
- Add finely chopped onion, carrots, celery, and minced garlic to the skillet. Cook for 5-7 minutes until the vegetables are softened.

Season and Add Tomatoes:
- Stir in dried oregano, dried basil, and red pepper flakes (if using). Pour in the crushed tomatoes and red wine (if using). Season with salt and black pepper to taste.

Simmer:
- Bring the mixture to a simmer, then reduce the heat to low. Allow the Bolognese sauce to simmer for 15-20 minutes to let the flavors meld and the sauce thicken.

Adjust Seasoning:

- Taste the sauce and adjust the seasoning if needed. Add more salt, pepper, or herbs according to your preference.

Cook Pasta:
- While the sauce is simmering, cook the pasta according to the package instructions. Drain and set aside.

Serve:
- Serve the Quick Beef Bolognese over the cooked pasta.
- Garnish with chopped fresh parsley and grated Parmesan cheese.

Enjoy:
- Enjoy this quick and flavorful Beef Bolognese for a satisfying and comforting meal!

This quick and easy Beef Bolognese is perfect for a busy weeknight. The combination of ground beef, aromatic vegetables, and rich tomato sauce creates a delicious and hearty pasta dish. Serve it over your favorite pasta for a comforting and flavorful meal.

Beef and Noodle Stir-Fry

Ingredients:

For the Beef Marinade:

- 1 lb (450g) beef sirloin or flank, thinly sliced
- 2 tablespoons soy sauce
- 1 tablespoon oyster sauce
- 1 tablespoon hoisin sauce
- 1 tablespoon sesame oil
- 1 teaspoon sugar
- 1/2 teaspoon black pepper
- 1 tablespoon cornstarch

For the Stir-Fry:

- 8 oz (225g) egg noodles or rice noodles
- 2 tablespoons vegetable oil
- 3 cloves garlic, minced
- 1 tablespoon fresh ginger, grated
- 1 bell pepper, thinly sliced
- 1 carrot, julienned
- 1 cup broccoli florets
- 1/2 cup snow peas, trimmed
- 1/4 cup soy sauce
- 1 tablespoon oyster sauce
- 1 tablespoon hoisin sauce
- 1 tablespoon rice vinegar
- 1 tablespoon sesame oil
- Green onions, sliced (for garnish)
- Sesame seeds (for garnish, optional)

Instructions:

Prepare the Beef:

- In a bowl, combine thinly sliced beef with soy sauce, oyster sauce, hoisin sauce, sesame oil, sugar, black pepper, and cornstarch. Allow it to marinate for at least 15-20 minutes.

Cook the Noodles:
- Cook the egg or rice noodles according to the package instructions. Drain and set aside.

Stir-Fry the Beef:
- Heat vegetable oil in a wok or large skillet over high heat.
- Add the marinated beef slices and stir-fry for 2-3 minutes until they are browned and cooked through. Remove the beef from the wok and set it aside.

Cook the Vegetables:
- In the same wok, add a bit more oil if needed. Stir-fry minced garlic and grated ginger for about 30 seconds until aromatic.
- Add thinly sliced bell pepper, julienned carrot, broccoli florets, and snow peas to the wok. Stir-fry for 3-4 minutes until the vegetables are crisp-tender.

Combine Beef and Vegetables:
- Return the cooked beef to the wok with the sautéed vegetables. Mix everything together.

Prepare the Sauce:
- In a small bowl, whisk together soy sauce, oyster sauce, hoisin sauce, rice vinegar, and sesame oil.
- Pour the sauce over the beef and vegetable mixture. Stir to coat everything evenly.

Add Noodles:
- Add the cooked and drained noodles to the wok. Toss and stir to combine, ensuring the noodles are well coated with the sauce.

Garnish and Serve:
- Garnish the Beef and Noodle Stir-Fry with sliced green onions and sesame seeds if desired.

Enjoy:
- Serve immediately and enjoy this delicious and satisfying Beef and Noodle Stir-Fry!

This flavorful and colorful Beef and Noodle Stir-Fry is a quick and delicious meal that combines tender beef, crisp vegetables, and perfectly cooked noodles. The savory and slightly sweet sauce enhances the overall taste, making it a great option for a quick weeknight dinner.

Beef Quesadillas

Ingredients:

For the Beef Filling:

- 1 lb (450g) ground beef
- 1 small onion, finely chopped
- 2 cloves garlic, minced
- 1 teaspoon ground cumin
- 1 teaspoon chili powder
- 1/2 teaspoon paprika
- Salt and black pepper to taste
- 1/4 cup water (if needed)

For the Quesadillas:

- 8 medium-sized flour tortillas
- 2 cups shredded cheese (cheddar, Monterey Jack, or a blend)
- 1 cup diced tomatoes
- 1/2 cup chopped fresh cilantro
- Sour cream and salsa (for serving)

Instructions:

Cook the Beef Filling:
- In a skillet over medium heat, cook ground beef until browned. Drain excess fat.
- Add finely chopped onion and minced garlic to the skillet. Cook until the onion is softened.
- Season the beef with ground cumin, chili powder, paprika, salt, and black pepper. If the mixture becomes too dry, add a bit of water to keep it moist. Cook for an additional 2-3 minutes until well combined.

Assemble the Quesadillas:
- Place a tortilla on a flat surface.
- Sprinkle a portion of shredded cheese on one half of the tortilla.
- Spoon some of the beef filling over the cheese.
- Add diced tomatoes and chopped cilantro on top.
- Fold the tortilla in half, creating a semi-circle shape.

Cook the Quesadillas:
- Heat a large skillet or griddle over medium heat.
- Place the assembled quesadilla on the skillet and cook for 2-3 minutes on each side, or until the tortilla is golden brown and the cheese is melted.
- Repeat the process for the remaining tortillas and filling.

Serve:
- Slice the cooked quesadillas into wedges.
- Serve with sour cream and salsa on the side for dipping.

Enjoy:
- Enjoy these delicious Beef Quesadillas as a quick and flavorful meal or snack!

Beef Quesadillas are a versatile and crowd-pleasing dish that's perfect for a quick lunch, dinner, or party appetizer. The combination of seasoned ground beef, melted cheese, and fresh toppings creates a tasty and satisfying treat. Customize with your favorite ingredients and serve with your preferred dipping sauces for a delightful experience.

Mongolian Beef

Ingredients:

For the Beef Marinade:

- 1 lb (450g) flank steak, thinly sliced
- 1/4 cup soy sauce
- 1 tablespoon cornstarch
- 1 tablespoon vegetable oil

For the Sauce:

- 1/2 cup soy sauce
- 1/2 cup water
- 1/2 cup brown sugar, packed
- 2 tablespoons hoisin sauce
- 2 tablespoons rice vinegar
- 1 teaspoon sesame oil

For Cooking:

- 2 tablespoons vegetable oil
- 3 cloves garlic, minced
- 1 tablespoon fresh ginger, grated
- 2 green onions, sliced (white and green parts separated)
- 1 tablespoon cornstarch mixed with 2 tablespoons water (slurry)

For Garnish:

- Sesame seeds (optional)
- Sliced green onions (green parts)

Instructions:

Marinate the Beef:

- In a bowl, combine thinly sliced flank steak with soy sauce, cornstarch, and vegetable oil. Allow it to marinate for at least 15-20 minutes.

Prepare the Sauce:
- In another bowl, whisk together soy sauce, water, brown sugar, hoisin sauce, rice vinegar, and sesame oil to create the sauce. Set aside.

Cook the Beef:
- Heat vegetable oil in a wok or large skillet over high heat.
- Add the marinated beef slices and stir-fry for 2-3 minutes until browned and cooked through. Remove the beef from the wok and set it aside.

Saute Aromatics:
- In the same wok, add a bit more oil if needed. Stir-fry minced garlic, grated ginger, and the white parts of the sliced green onions for about 30 seconds until aromatic.

Combine Beef and Sauce:
- Return the cooked beef to the wok with the sautéed aromatics.
- Pour the prepared sauce over the beef and stir to coat everything evenly.

Thicken the Sauce:
- Stir in the cornstarch slurry and continue to cook for an additional 1-2 minutes until the sauce thickens.

Garnish and Serve:
- Garnish the Mongolian Beef with sesame seeds (if using) and sliced green onions (green parts).
- Serve the dish over steamed rice or noodles.

Enjoy:
- Enjoy this flavorful and tender Mongolian Beef for a delicious and satisfying meal!

Mongolian Beef is a classic Chinese-American dish known for its sweet and savory flavors. This homemade version allows you to control the ingredients and enjoy the delicious combination of tender beef slices in a rich and flavorful sauce. Serve it with your favorite side for a complete and tasty meal.

Beef and Vegetable Kabobs

Ingredients:

For the Marinade:

- 1.5 lbs (680g) beef sirloin or tenderloin, cut into 1-inch cubes
- 1/4 cup soy sauce
- 2 tablespoons olive oil
- 2 tablespoons balsamic vinegar
- 2 tablespoons honey
- 3 cloves garlic, minced
- 1 teaspoon Dijon mustard
- 1 teaspoon dried rosemary
- Salt and black pepper to taste

For the Kabobs:

- Cherry tomatoes
- Bell peppers (red, yellow, and green), cut into chunks
- Red onion, cut into chunks
- Zucchini, sliced into rounds
- Mushrooms, cleaned and halved
- Metal or wooden skewers (if using wooden skewers, soak them in water for 30 minutes before threading)

Instructions:

Prepare the Marinade:
- In a bowl, whisk together soy sauce, olive oil, balsamic vinegar, honey, minced garlic, Dijon mustard, dried rosemary, salt, and black pepper.

Marinate the Beef:
- Place the beef cubes in a shallow dish or a resealable plastic bag.
- Pour the marinade over the beef, ensuring it's well coated. Marinate for at least 30 minutes to 2 hours in the refrigerator.

Assemble the Kabobs:
- Preheat the grill or grill pan to medium-high heat.

- Thread marinated beef cubes onto skewers, alternating with cherry tomatoes, bell peppers, red onion, zucchini, and mushrooms.

Grill the Kabobs:
- Place the assembled kabobs on the preheated grill.
- Grill for 8-10 minutes, turning occasionally, or until the beef reaches your desired level of doneness and the vegetables are tender and slightly charred.

Serve:
- Remove the kabobs from the grill and let them rest for a few minutes.
- Serve the Beef and Vegetable Kabobs hot, either on or off the skewers.

Enjoy:
- Enjoy these flavorful and colorful Beef and Vegetable Kabobs as a delicious and satisfying meal!

Beef and Vegetable Kabobs are a fantastic option for a summertime barbecue or a quick and healthy dinner. The marinated beef becomes tender and flavorful, while the assortment of grilled vegetables adds vibrant colors and textures. Serve these kabobs with your favorite side dishes or a refreshing salad for a complete and delightful meal.

Beef and Black Bean Stir-Fry

Ingredients:

For the Marinade:

- 1 lb (450g) beef sirloin or flank, thinly sliced
- 2 tablespoons soy sauce
- 1 tablespoon oyster sauce
- 1 tablespoon hoisin sauce
- 1 tablespoon rice wine or dry sherry
- 1 tablespoon cornstarch
- 1 teaspoon sesame oil
- 1 teaspoon sugar
- 1/2 teaspoon black pepper

For the Stir-Fry:

- 2 tablespoons vegetable oil
- 3 cloves garlic, minced
- 1 tablespoon fresh ginger, grated
- 1 bell pepper, thinly sliced
- 1 carrot, julienned
- 1 cup snap peas, trimmed
- 1 can (15 oz) black beans, drained and rinsed
- 2 green onions, sliced (white and green parts separated)
- Cooked rice (for serving)

Instructions:

Marinate the Beef:
- In a bowl, combine thinly sliced beef with soy sauce, oyster sauce, hoisin sauce, rice wine or dry sherry, cornstarch, sesame oil, sugar, and black pepper. Allow it to marinate for at least 15-20 minutes.

Prepare the Stir-Fry:
- Heat vegetable oil in a wok or large skillet over high heat.

- Add minced garlic and grated ginger to the wok. Stir-fry for about 30 seconds until aromatic.

Cook the Beef:
- Add the marinated beef to the wok and stir-fry for 2-3 minutes until browned and cooked through. Remove the beef from the wok and set it aside.

Stir-Fry Vegetables:
- In the same wok, add a bit more oil if needed. Stir-fry thinly sliced bell pepper, julienned carrot, and snap peas for 3-4 minutes until they are crisp-tender.

Combine Beef, Vegetables, and Black Beans:
- Return the cooked beef to the wok with the sautéed vegetables.
- Add drained and rinsed black beans and sliced green onions (white parts). Stir to combine.

Serve:
- Serve the Beef and Black Bean Stir-Fry over cooked rice.
- Garnish with sliced green onions (green parts).

Enjoy:
- Enjoy this quick and flavorful Beef and Black Bean Stir-Fry for a delicious and satisfying meal!

Beef and Black Bean Stir-Fry is a savory and satisfying dish that combines tender beef, crisp vegetables, and hearty black beans. The marinated beef adds depth of flavor, and the combination of ingredients creates a well-balanced and tasty stir-fry. Serve it over rice for a complete and delightful meal.

Comfort Food Classics:

Beef Pot Roast

Ingredients:

- 3-4 lbs (1.4-1.8 kg) beef chuck roast
- Salt and black pepper to taste
- 2 tablespoons vegetable oil
- 1 large onion, sliced
- 3 cloves garlic, minced
- 2 carrots, peeled and cut into large chunks
- 3 celery stalks, cut into large chunks
- 2 cups beef broth
- 1 cup red wine (or additional beef broth)
- 2 tablespoons tomato paste
- 2 teaspoons Worcestershire sauce
- 1 teaspoon dried thyme
- 2 bay leaves
- 4-5 potatoes, peeled and cut into chunks
- 4-5 carrots, peeled and cut into chunks
- Fresh parsley for garnish (optional)

Instructions:

Preheat and Season:
- Preheat your oven to 325°F (163°C).
- Season the beef chuck roast generously with salt and black pepper.

Sear the Roast:
- Heat vegetable oil in a large Dutch oven or oven-safe pot over medium-high heat.
- Sear the seasoned roast on all sides until browned. This helps to lock in the flavors.

Saute Aromatics:
- Add sliced onions to the pot and sauté until they are softened.
- Add minced garlic and cook for about 30 seconds until fragrant.

Add Liquids and Flavorings:

- Pour in beef broth and red wine (or additional beef broth) to deglaze the pot, scraping up any browned bits from the bottom.
- Stir in tomato paste, Worcestershire sauce, dried thyme, and add bay leaves for flavor.

Braise in the Oven:
- Place the seared roast back into the pot. Cover the pot with a lid and transfer it to the preheated oven.
- Allow the roast to braise for about 2 to 2.5 hours, or until the meat is fork-tender.

Add Vegetables:
- After the initial braising time, add chunks of potatoes, carrots, and celery to the pot.
- Continue to cook for an additional 45 minutes to 1 hour, or until the vegetables are tender.

Check and Adjust:
- Check the seasoning and adjust with salt and pepper if needed.
- Remove bay leaves before serving.

Serve:
- Carefully remove the pot from the oven.
- Serve the Beef Pot Roast with the vegetables, garnished with fresh parsley if desired.

Enjoy:
- Enjoy this comforting and flavorful Beef Pot Roast as a hearty and classic family meal!

This classic Beef Pot Roast recipe results in a tender and succulent dish with rich flavors. The slow braising process allows the meat to become melt-in-your-mouth tender, and the addition of vegetables creates a complete and satisfying meal. Perfect for family gatherings or cozy dinners.

Beef and Potato Casserole

Ingredients:

- 1.5 lbs (680g) ground beef
- 1 onion, finely chopped
- 3 cloves garlic, minced
- 1 teaspoon dried thyme
- Salt and black pepper to taste
- 2 tablespoons tomato paste
- 1 cup beef broth
- 4 cups potatoes, thinly sliced (about 4 medium-sized potatoes)
- 1 cup shredded cheddar cheese
- 1/2 cup sour cream
- 2 tablespoons unsalted butter, melted
- Fresh parsley, chopped (for garnish, optional)

Instructions:

Preheat the Oven:
- Preheat your oven to 375°F (190°C).

Cook the Ground Beef:
- In a large skillet over medium-high heat, cook ground beef until browned, breaking it apart with a spoon. Drain excess fat.

Saute Aromatics:
- Add finely chopped onion and minced garlic to the skillet. Sauté until the onion is softened.

Season and Add Tomato Paste:
- Season the beef mixture with dried thyme, salt, and black pepper.
- Stir in tomato paste and cook for an additional 2-3 minutes.

Add Beef Broth:
- Pour in beef broth, stirring to combine. Let it simmer for a few minutes to allow the flavors to meld.

Layer Potatoes and Beef Mixture:
- In a greased baking dish, layer half of the thinly sliced potatoes.
- Spoon half of the beef mixture over the potatoes.
- Repeat the layers with the remaining potatoes and beef mixture.

Combine Cheese and Sour Cream:
- In a bowl, combine shredded cheddar cheese and sour cream.

- Spread this mixture evenly over the top layer of beef.

Drizzle with Melted Butter:
- Drizzle melted butter over the top.

Bake in the Oven:
- Cover the baking dish with aluminum foil and bake for 45 minutes.
- Remove the foil and bake for an additional 15-20 minutes, or until the potatoes are tender, and the top is golden brown.

Garnish and Serve:
- Garnish the Beef and Potato Casserole with chopped fresh parsley if desired.

Enjoy:
- Serve this comforting and hearty Beef and Potato Casserole as a delicious and satisfying meal!

This casserole brings together layers of seasoned ground beef, thinly sliced potatoes, and a cheesy sour cream topping. It bakes to perfection, resulting in a hearty and comforting dish. Enjoy it as a family-friendly dinner or bring it to gatherings for a crowd-pleasing meal.

Beef and Guinness Pie

Ingredients:

For the Filling:

- 2 lbs (900g) stewing beef, cut into chunks
- 2 tablespoons vegetable oil
- 2 onions, chopped
- 3 cloves garlic, minced
- 2 carrots, peeled and diced
- 2 celery stalks, diced
- 1 cup mushrooms, sliced
- 2 tablespoons all-purpose flour
- 1 can (14.9 oz) Guinness stout
- 2 cups beef broth
- 2 tablespoons tomato paste
- 2 teaspoons Worcestershire sauce
- 2 teaspoons dried thyme
- Salt and black pepper to taste

For the Pastry:

- 2 sheets of store-bought puff pastry, thawed
- 1 egg, beaten (for egg wash)

Instructions:

Preheat Oven:
- Preheat your oven to 375°F (190°C).

Brown the Beef:
- In a large oven-safe pot or Dutch oven, heat vegetable oil over medium-high heat.
- Brown the stewing beef chunks in batches until they are well-seared. Remove and set aside.

Saute Vegetables:

- In the same pot, add chopped onions, minced garlic, diced carrots, diced celery, and sliced mushrooms. Cook until the vegetables are softened.

Add Flour and Deglaze:
- Sprinkle flour over the sautéed vegetables and stir to coat.
- Pour in Guinness stout to deglaze the pot, scraping up any browned bits from the bottom.

Combine Ingredients:
- Return the seared beef to the pot.
- Add beef broth, tomato paste, Worcestershire sauce, dried thyme, salt, and black pepper. Stir to combine.

Simmer:
- Bring the mixture to a simmer. Cover the pot and transfer it to the preheated oven.
- Allow the stew to cook in the oven for 2 to 2.5 hours, or until the beef is tender.

Prepare Pastry:
- Remove the pot from the oven. Increase the oven temperature to 400°F (204°C).
- Roll out the puff pastry sheets on a lightly floured surface to fit the size of your pot.

Assemble and Bake:
- Place the rolled-out puff pastry over the stew in the pot, covering the filling completely.
- Brush the pastry with beaten egg for a golden finish.
- Cut a few slits in the pastry to allow steam to escape.
- Transfer the pot to the oven and bake for about 20-25 minutes or until the pastry is golden brown and puffed.

Serve:
- Remove the Beef and Guinness Pie from the oven.
- Serve hot, scooping out portions of the savory beef filling with the flaky puff pastry.

Enjoy:
- Enjoy this hearty and flavorful Beef and Guinness Pie as a comforting and delicious meal!

This Beef and Guinness Pie is a classic savory dish with rich flavors and a golden, flaky pastry topping. It's perfect for colder weather or when you crave a hearty and satisfying meal. Serve it with your favorite sides for a complete and comforting dining experience.

Stuffed Bell Peppers with Ground Beef

Ingredients:

- 6 large bell peppers (any color)
- 1 lb (450g) ground beef
- 1 cup cooked rice
- 1 onion, finely chopped
- 2 cloves garlic, minced
- 1 can (14.5 oz) diced tomatoes, drained
- 1 cup black beans, drained and rinsed
- 1 cup corn kernels (fresh or frozen)
- 1 teaspoon ground cumin
- 1 teaspoon chili powder
- Salt and black pepper to taste
- 1 cup shredded cheddar cheese
- Fresh cilantro or parsley for garnish (optional)
- Salsa and sour cream (for serving)

Instructions:

Preheat Oven:
- Preheat your oven to 375°F (190°C).

Prepare Bell Peppers:
- Cut the tops off the bell peppers and remove the seeds and membranes. If needed, trim the bottoms slightly to help them stand upright in the baking dish.
- Place the bell peppers in a baking dish.

Cook Ground Beef:
- In a skillet over medium heat, cook ground beef until browned. Drain excess fat if necessary.

Saute Aromatics:
- Add chopped onion and minced garlic to the skillet with the cooked beef. Cook until the onion is softened.

Combine Ingredients:
- In a large bowl, combine the cooked beef and onion mixture with cooked rice, diced tomatoes, black beans, corn, ground cumin, chili powder, salt, and black pepper. Mix well.

Stuff Bell Peppers:
- Spoon the beef and rice mixture into each bell pepper, pressing down gently to pack the filling.

Top with Cheese:
- Sprinkle shredded cheddar cheese on top of each stuffed pepper.

Bake:
- Cover the baking dish with aluminum foil.
- Bake in the preheated oven for 25-30 minutes or until the peppers are tender.

Broil (Optional):
- If you want a golden and bubbly cheese topping, remove the foil and broil for an additional 2-3 minutes until the cheese is melted and lightly browned.

Serve:
- Remove the stuffed bell peppers from the oven.
- Garnish with fresh cilantro or parsley if desired.

Enjoy:
- Serve the Stuffed Bell Peppers with Ground Beef hot, accompanied by salsa and sour cream on the side.

These Stuffed Bell Peppers with Ground Beef are a satisfying and flavorful meal. The combination of seasoned ground beef, rice, vegetables, and melted cheese creates a hearty and comforting dish. Customize the filling to suit your taste, and enjoy this classic recipe for a delicious and nutritious dinner.

Beef and Vegetable Stew

Ingredients:

- 2 lbs (900g) beef stew meat, cut into bite-sized pieces
- 2 tablespoons vegetable oil
- 1 large onion, chopped
- 3 cloves garlic, minced
- 4 cups beef broth
- 1 cup red wine (optional)
- 2 tablespoons tomato paste
- 2 bay leaves
- 1 teaspoon dried thyme
- Salt and black pepper to taste
- 4 carrots, peeled and sliced
- 3 potatoes, peeled and diced
- 2 celery stalks, sliced
- 1 cup frozen peas
- 1 cup frozen green beans
- Fresh parsley for garnish (optional)

Instructions:

Brown the Beef:
- In a large pot or Dutch oven, heat vegetable oil over medium-high heat.
- Brown the beef stew meat in batches, ensuring all sides are seared. Remove the browned meat and set it aside.

Saute Aromatics:
- In the same pot, add chopped onions and sauté until they are softened.
- Add minced garlic and cook for about 30 seconds until fragrant.

Deglaze and Add Ingredients:
- Pour in beef broth and red wine (if using) to deglaze the pot, scraping up any browned bits from the bottom.
- Stir in tomato paste, bay leaves, dried thyme, salt, and black pepper.

Simmer:
- Return the browned beef to the pot. Bring the mixture to a simmer.
- Cover the pot with a lid and let it simmer on low heat for about 1.5 to 2 hours, or until the beef is tender.

Add Vegetables:
- Add sliced carrots, diced potatoes, and sliced celery to the pot.
- Continue to simmer until the vegetables are tender, usually 20-30 minutes.

Add Frozen Vegetables:
- Stir in frozen peas and green beans. Cook for an additional 5-10 minutes until they are heated through.

Check and Adjust Seasoning:
- Taste the stew and adjust the seasoning if needed. Add more salt and pepper according to your preference.

Serve:
- Remove bay leaves from the stew.
- Ladle the Beef and Vegetable Stew into bowls.

Garnish and Enjoy:
- Garnish with fresh parsley if desired.
- Enjoy this hearty and comforting Beef and Vegetable Stew on a cold day!

This Beef and Vegetable Stew is a wholesome and comforting dish that's perfect for chilly days. The combination of tender beef, flavorful broth, and a variety of vegetables creates a satisfying and nutritious meal. Serve it with crusty bread or over mashed potatoes for a complete and hearty experience.

Beef Shepherd's Pie

Ingredients:

For the Filling:

- 1.5 lbs (680g) ground beef
- 1 onion, finely chopped
- 2 cloves garlic, minced
- 2 carrots, diced
- 1 cup frozen peas
- 1 cup corn kernels (fresh or frozen)
- 2 tablespoons tomato paste
- 2 tablespoons all-purpose flour
- 1 cup beef broth
- 1 tablespoon Worcestershire sauce
- 1 teaspoon dried thyme
- Salt and black pepper to taste

For the Mashed Potato Topping:

- 4 large potatoes, peeled and diced
- 1/2 cup milk
- 4 tablespoons butter
- Salt and black pepper to taste
- 1 cup shredded cheddar cheese (optional, for topping)

Instructions:

Preheat Oven:
- Preheat your oven to 400°F (200°C).

Prepare Potatoes:
- Boil or steam the diced potatoes until they are fork-tender.
- Mash the potatoes with milk, butter, salt, and black pepper until smooth and creamy.

Cook the Filling:

- In a large skillet, brown the ground beef over medium heat. Drain excess fat if necessary.
- Add chopped onions, minced garlic, and diced carrots to the skillet. Cook until the onions are softened.
- Stir in tomato paste and flour, coating the meat and vegetables.
- Pour in beef broth and Worcestershire sauce. Add frozen peas, corn, dried thyme, salt, and black pepper. Stir well.
- Allow the mixture to simmer for 10-15 minutes until it thickens.

Assemble Shepherd's Pie:
- Transfer the beef filling to a baking dish, spreading it evenly.
- Spoon the mashed potatoes over the beef filling, smoothing the top with a spatula.

Optional Cheese Topping:
- If desired, sprinkle shredded cheddar cheese over the mashed potatoes.

Bake:
- Place the baking dish in the preheated oven.
- Bake for 20-25 minutes or until the top is golden brown and the filling is bubbly.

Serve:
- Remove the Beef Shepherd's Pie from the oven.
- Allow it to cool slightly before serving.

Enjoy:
- Serve this comforting and hearty Beef Shepherd's Pie, enjoying the layers of flavorful beef and vegetables topped with creamy mashed potatoes.

Beef Shepherd's Pie is a classic and satisfying dish that combines a savory ground beef filling with a layer of creamy mashed potatoes. It's a comforting and complete meal in one dish. Customize the filling with your favorite vegetables and herbs for a delicious family dinner.

Corned Beef and Cabbage

Ingredients:

- 1 corned beef brisket (about 3-4 pounds), with spice packet
- 8 small red potatoes, halved
- 4 large carrots, peeled and cut into chunks
- 1 small head of cabbage, cut into wedges
- 1 onion, peeled and quartered
- 4 cloves garlic, minced
- 1 bay leaf
- Water
- Mustard (for serving)

Instructions:

Prepare the Corned Beef:
- Rinse the corned beef brisket under cold water.
- Place the corned beef in a large pot or Dutch oven. Add the spice packet that comes with the corned beef.
- Cover the corned beef with water, making sure it is fully submerged.

Simmer:
- Bring the water to a boil, then reduce the heat to a simmer.
- Cover and let the corned beef simmer for about 3 hours or until it is tender. Skim off any foam that rises to the surface.

Add Vegetables:
- After the corned beef has simmered for about 2 hours, add halved red potatoes, carrot chunks, quartered onion, minced garlic, and a bay leaf to the pot.
- Continue to simmer for another hour or until the vegetables are tender.

Add Cabbage:
- In the last 15-20 minutes of cooking, add the cabbage wedges to the pot. They should be cooked until they are tender but not overly soft.

Slice and Serve:
- Once everything is cooked, remove the corned beef from the pot and let it rest for a few minutes.
- Slice the corned beef against the grain into thin slices.
- Arrange the sliced corned beef, vegetables, and cabbage on a serving platter.

Serve:
- Serve the Corned Beef and Cabbage with mustard on the side.

Enjoy:
- Enjoy this classic Irish dish as a hearty and comforting meal!

Corned Beef and Cabbage is a traditional Irish dish often associated with St. Patrick's Day, but it's delicious any time of the year. The slow simmering of the corned beef with flavorful spices and the addition of hearty vegetables makes for a satisfying and comforting meal.

Sloppy Joes

Ingredients:

- 1 lb (450g) ground beef
- 1 small onion, finely chopped
- 1 bell pepper, finely chopped
- 2 cloves garlic, minced
- 1/2 cup ketchup
- 2 tablespoons tomato paste
- 1 tablespoon brown sugar
- 1 tablespoon Worcestershire sauce
- 1 teaspoon Dijon mustard
- 1/2 teaspoon chili powder
- 1/2 teaspoon paprika
- Salt and black pepper to taste
- Hamburger buns

Instructions:

Cook Ground Beef:
- In a large skillet over medium heat, cook the ground beef, breaking it apart with a spatula, until browned and cooked through.

Saute Vegetables:
- Add chopped onions and bell peppers to the skillet with the cooked beef. Cook until the vegetables are softened.

Add Aromatics:
- Stir in minced garlic and cook for about 30 seconds until fragrant.

Combine Sauce Ingredients:
- In a bowl, whisk together ketchup, tomato paste, brown sugar, Worcestershire sauce, Dijon mustard, chili powder, paprika, salt, and black pepper.

Add Sauce to Skillet:
- Pour the sauce mixture over the cooked beef and vegetables in the skillet.
- Stir to combine, ensuring that the meat and vegetables are coated in the sauce.

Simmer:
- Reduce the heat to low and let the mixture simmer for about 10-15 minutes, allowing the flavors to meld and the sauce to thicken.

Toast Buns:
- While the Sloppy Joe mixture is simmering, you can toast the hamburger buns.
- Place the buns in a toaster or oven until they are lightly toasted.

Serve:
- Spoon the Sloppy Joe mixture onto the toasted buns.

Enjoy:
- Enjoy these classic Sloppy Joes, either open-faced or as a sandwich, for a quick and satisfying meal!

Sloppy Joes are a simple and flavorful dish that's perfect for a quick weeknight dinner. The combination of savory ground beef, sweet and tangy sauce, and crunchy vegetables makes for a delicious and messy sandwich. Customize the recipe with your favorite spices and serve it with your preferred side dishes for a tasty and family-friendly meal.

Beef and Mushroom Pie

Ingredients:

For the Filling:

- 1.5 lbs (680g) beef stew meat, cut into bite-sized pieces
- 2 tablespoons vegetable oil
- 1 onion, finely chopped
- 2 cloves garlic, minced
- 8 oz (225g) mushrooms, sliced
- 2 tablespoons all-purpose flour
- 1 cup beef broth
- 1 cup red wine (optional)
- 2 tablespoons tomato paste
- 1 teaspoon Worcestershire sauce
- 1 teaspoon dried thyme
- Salt and black pepper to taste

For the Pastry:

- 2 sheets of store-bought puff pastry, thawed
- 1 egg, beaten (for egg wash)

Instructions:

Preheat Oven:
- Preheat your oven to 400°F (200°C).

Brown the Beef:
- In a large skillet, heat vegetable oil over medium-high heat.
- Brown the beef stew meat in batches until it's well-seared. Remove and set aside.

Saute Aromatics:
- In the same skillet, add chopped onions and minced garlic. Cook until the onions are softened.
- Add sliced mushrooms and cook until they release their moisture and become golden brown.

Add Flour and Deglaze:
- Sprinkle flour over the mushroom mixture and stir to coat.
- Pour in beef broth and red wine (if using) to deglaze the skillet, scraping up any browned bits from the bottom.

Combine Ingredients:
- Return the seared beef to the skillet. Stir in tomato paste, Worcestershire sauce, dried thyme, salt, and black pepper.

Simmer:
- Allow the mixture to simmer until the sauce thickens and the beef is tender. This will take about 15-20 minutes.

Prepare Pastry:
- While the filling is simmering, roll out the puff pastry sheets on a lightly floured surface to fit the size of your pie dish.

Assemble Pie:
- Transfer the beef and mushroom filling to a pie dish.
- Place the rolled-out puff pastry over the filling, ensuring it covers the entire surface.

Brush with Egg Wash:
- Brush the pastry with beaten egg for a golden finish.

Cut Slits:
- Make a few slits in the pastry to allow steam to escape.

Bake:
- Place the pie dish in the preheated oven.
- Bake for 20-25 minutes or until the pastry is golden brown and puffed.

Serve:
- Remove the Beef and Mushroom Pie from the oven.
- Allow it to cool slightly before serving.

Enjoy:
- Serve this savory and comforting Beef and Mushroom Pie as a delicious and hearty meal!

This Beef and Mushroom Pie is a flavorful and comforting dish with tender beef, earthy mushrooms, and a golden, flaky pastry crust. It's perfect for a cozy family dinner or a special occasion. Customize the filling with your favorite herbs and enjoy the rich and satisfying flavors of this classic savory pie.

Philly Cheesesteak Sandwich

Ingredients:

For the Steak:

- 1 lb (450g) thinly sliced ribeye or sirloin steak
- Salt and black pepper to taste
- 2 tablespoons vegetable oil
- 1 large onion, thinly sliced
- 1 bell pepper (green or red), thinly sliced

For the Sandwich:

- 4 hoagie rolls or sub rolls
- 8 slices provolone cheese
- Optional toppings: sautéed mushrooms, pickled jalapeños, mayonnaise, ketchup

Instructions:

Preheat Grill or Skillet:
- Preheat a grill or a large skillet over medium-high heat.

Season and Cook the Steak:
- Season the thinly sliced steak with salt and black pepper.
- In the hot skillet or on the grill, cook the steak slices for 1-2 minutes on each side or until they are browned and cooked to your liking.
- Remove the steak from the skillet or grill and set it aside.

Sauté Onions and Peppers:
- In the same skillet, add vegetable oil.
- Add thinly sliced onions and bell peppers. Sauté until they are softened and slightly caramelized.

Combine Steak, Onions, and Peppers:
- Return the cooked steak slices to the skillet with the sautéed onions and peppers.
- Toss everything together to combine and heat through.

Melt Cheese:
- Place slices of provolone cheese over the steak, onions, and peppers.

- Cover the skillet with a lid or foil and let the cheese melt for a minute or two.

Prepare Rolls:
- While the cheese is melting, lightly toast the hoagie rolls in the oven or on the grill.

Assemble Sandwiches:
- Spoon the cheesy steak mixture onto the toasted hoagie rolls.
- Optionally, add toppings such as sautéed mushrooms, pickled jalapeños, mayonnaise, or ketchup.

Serve:
- Serve the Philly Cheesesteak Sandwiches hot and enjoy!

Philly Cheesesteak Sandwiches are a classic and delicious treat, featuring thinly sliced steak, sautéed onions and peppers, and gooey melted cheese, all nestled in a toasted hoagie roll. This iconic sandwich is a crowd-pleaser and perfect for a quick and satisfying meal. Customize it with your favorite toppings and enjoy the authentic flavors of a Philly Cheesesteak at home!

Fusion and Creative Twists:

Beef and Shrimp Spring Rolls

Ingredients:

For the Filling:

- 8-10 spring roll rice paper wrappers
- 1/2 lb (225g) cooked shrimp, peeled and deveined
- 1/2 lb (225g) thinly sliced beef (sirloin or flank)
- 1 cup rice vermicelli noodles, cooked according to package instructions
- 1 cup shredded lettuce
- 1 cup bean sprouts
- 1 cucumber, julienned
- Fresh mint leaves
- Fresh cilantro leaves
- 1/4 cup chopped peanuts (optional)

For the Dipping Sauce:

- 1/4 cup hoisin sauce
- 2 tablespoons soy sauce
- 1 tablespoon rice vinegar
- 1 tablespoon sweet chili sauce
- 1 clove garlic, minced
- 1 teaspoon sesame oil

Instructions:

Prepare Filling Ingredients:
- Cook rice vermicelli noodles according to package instructions and set aside.
- Peel and devein cooked shrimp.
- Thinly slice beef and prepare all vegetables and herbs.

Dipping Sauce:

- In a small bowl, whisk together hoisin sauce, soy sauce, rice vinegar, sweet chili sauce, minced garlic, and sesame oil. Set aside.

Prepare Rice Paper Wrappers:
- Fill a shallow dish with warm water.
- Dip one rice paper wrapper into the water for about 5-10 seconds until it softens.
- Place the softened wrapper on a clean surface.

Assemble Spring Rolls:
- In the center of the wrapper, layer a few slices of beef, shrimp, a handful of rice vermicelli noodles, shredded lettuce, bean sprouts, cucumber, mint leaves, and cilantro.
- Optionally, sprinkle chopped peanuts on top.

Roll Spring Rolls:
- Fold the sides of the wrapper over the filling, then fold the bottom up and roll tightly.
- Repeat the process until all the filling is used.

Serve:
- Serve the Beef and Shrimp Spring Rolls immediately with the prepared dipping sauce.
- Optionally, you can cut the spring rolls in half diagonally before serving.

Enjoy:
- Enjoy these fresh and flavorful Beef and Shrimp Spring Rolls as a light and delicious appetizer or main dish!

Beef and Shrimp Spring Rolls are a delightful and healthy dish filled with a medley of fresh vegetables, succulent shrimp, and tender beef. The rice paper wrappers make them light and perfect for a refreshing appetizer or a light meal. Serve them with a tasty dipping sauce for an extra burst of flavor.

Beef and Sweet Potato Curry

Ingredients:

- 1.5 lbs (680g) beef stew meat, cubed
- 2 tablespoons vegetable oil
- 1 large onion, finely chopped
- 3 cloves garlic, minced
- 1 tablespoon fresh ginger, grated
- 2 tablespoons curry powder
- 1 teaspoon ground turmeric
- 1 teaspoon ground cumin
- 1 teaspoon ground coriander
- 1 teaspoon chili powder (adjust to taste)
- 1 can (14 oz) diced tomatoes
- 2 large sweet potatoes, peeled and diced
- 1 can (14 oz) coconut milk
- 1 cup beef or vegetable broth
- Salt and black pepper to taste
- Fresh cilantro, chopped (for garnish)
- Cooked rice (for serving)

Instructions:

Brown the Beef:
- In a large pot or Dutch oven, heat vegetable oil over medium-high heat.
- Brown the beef stew meat cubes in batches until they are well-seared on all sides. Remove and set aside.

Saute Aromatics:
- In the same pot, add finely chopped onions and cook until they are softened.
- Add minced garlic and grated ginger. Sauté for about 1 minute until fragrant.

Add Spices:
- Stir in curry powder, ground turmeric, ground cumin, ground coriander, and chili powder. Cook for 1-2 minutes to toast the spices.

Combine Ingredients:
- Return the browned beef to the pot.

- Add diced sweet potatoes, diced tomatoes (with juices), coconut milk, and beef or vegetable broth.
- Season with salt and black pepper to taste. Stir to combine.

Simmer:
- Bring the curry to a simmer. Cover the pot and let it simmer on low heat for about 1.5 to 2 hours, or until the beef and sweet potatoes are tender.

Adjust Seasoning:
- Taste the curry and adjust the seasoning if needed. Add more salt, pepper, or chili powder according to your preference.

Serve:
- Serve the Beef and Sweet Potato Curry over cooked rice.
- Garnish with chopped fresh cilantro.

Enjoy:
- Enjoy this hearty and flavorful Beef and Sweet Potato Curry for a satisfying and delicious meal!

This Beef and Sweet Potato Curry is a comforting and aromatic dish that combines tender beef, sweet potatoes, and a rich coconut curry sauce. The blend of spices adds depth and warmth to the dish, creating a satisfying and flavorful curry. Serve it over rice for a complete and delicious meal that's perfect for warming up on a chilly day.

Pineapple Beef Stir-Fry

Ingredients:

For the Stir-Fry:

- 1 lb (450g) beef sirloin or flank steak, thinly sliced
- 2 tablespoons soy sauce
- 1 tablespoon oyster sauce
- 1 tablespoon cornstarch
- 2 tablespoons vegetable oil, divided
- 1 bell pepper, thinly sliced
- 1 onion, thinly sliced
- 1 cup pineapple chunks (fresh or canned)
- 1 cup snap peas, ends trimmed
- 3 cloves garlic, minced
- 1 teaspoon fresh ginger, grated

For the Sauce:

- 1/4 cup pineapple juice
- 2 tablespoons soy sauce
- 1 tablespoon hoisin sauce
- 1 tablespoon rice vinegar
- 1 tablespoon brown sugar

Instructions:

Marinate the Beef:
- In a bowl, combine thinly sliced beef with soy sauce, oyster sauce, and cornstarch. Let it marinate for at least 15-20 minutes.

Prepare the Sauce:
- In a small bowl, whisk together pineapple juice, soy sauce, hoisin sauce, rice vinegar, and brown sugar. Set aside.

Stir-Fry Beef:
- Heat 1 tablespoon of vegetable oil in a wok or large skillet over high heat.

- Add the marinated beef and stir-fry for 2-3 minutes or until it is browned and cooked through. Remove the beef from the wok and set it aside.

Stir-Fry Vegetables:
- In the same wok, add another tablespoon of oil.
- Add thinly sliced bell pepper, onion, pineapple chunks, and snap peas. Stir-fry for 2-3 minutes until the vegetables are slightly tender but still crisp.

Add Aromatics:
- Add minced garlic and grated ginger to the vegetables. Stir-fry for an additional 1 minute until fragrant.

Combine Beef and Sauce:
- Return the cooked beef to the wok.
- Pour the prepared sauce over the beef and vegetables. Toss everything together to coat in the sauce.

Finish Cooking:
- Continue to stir-fry for another 2-3 minutes until everything is heated through and well-coated in the sauce.

Serve:
- Serve the Pineapple Beef Stir-Fry over cooked rice or noodles.
- Garnish with chopped green onions or cilantro if desired.

Enjoy:
- Enjoy this sweet and savory Pineapple Beef Stir-Fry for a delicious and quick meal with a tropical twist!

This Pineapple Beef Stir-Fry combines the sweetness of pineapple with savory beef and crisp vegetables for a delightful and flavorful dish. The quick stir-fry method ensures that the beef stays tender, and the pineapple-infused sauce adds a tropical touch. Serve it over rice or noodles for a complete and satisfying meal.

Beef and Blue Cheese Sliders

Ingredients:

For the Sliders:

- 1 lb (450g) ground beef
- Salt and black pepper to taste
- 1 tablespoon Worcestershire sauce
- 8 slider buns

For the Blue Cheese Sauce:

- 1/2 cup crumbled blue cheese
- 1/4 cup mayonnaise
- 2 tablespoons sour cream
- 1 tablespoon milk
- 1 teaspoon Dijon mustard
- Salt and black pepper to taste

For Toppings:

- Arugula or baby spinach leaves
- Sliced red onion (optional)
- Sliced tomatoes (optional)

Instructions:

Preheat Grill or Skillet:
- Preheat your grill or a skillet over medium-high heat.

Season and Shape Patties:
- In a bowl, combine ground beef, salt, black pepper, and Worcestershire sauce. Mix until well combined.
- Shape the seasoned beef mixture into small patties, slightly larger than the size of the slider buns.

Grill Patties:

- Grill the beef patties for about 3-4 minutes per side, or until they reach your desired level of doneness.
- Toast the slider buns on the grill for about 1-2 minutes until they are lightly golden.

Make Blue Cheese Sauce:
- In a separate bowl, combine crumbled blue cheese, mayonnaise, sour cream, milk, Dijon mustard, salt, and black pepper. Mix until smooth and well blended.

Assemble Sliders:
- Spread a dollop of blue cheese sauce on the bottom half of each slider bun.
- Place a grilled beef patty on top of the blue cheese sauce.
- Add arugula or baby spinach leaves on the patty.
- Optionally, add sliced red onion and sliced tomatoes.
- Top with the other half of the slider bun.

Serve:
- Serve the Beef and Blue Cheese Sliders immediately, and enjoy!

These Beef and Blue Cheese Sliders are perfect for a party or a delicious weeknight dinner. The combination of juicy beef patties, creamy blue cheese sauce, and fresh toppings creates a flavorful and satisfying bite. Customize the sliders with your favorite toppings and enjoy these tasty treats with family and friends.

Mediterranean Beef Skillet

Ingredients:

- 1.5 lbs (680g) lean ground beef
- 2 tablespoons olive oil
- 1 onion, finely chopped
- 3 cloves garlic, minced
- 1 teaspoon dried oregano
- 1 teaspoon dried basil
- 1 teaspoon dried thyme
- 1 teaspoon paprika
- Salt and black pepper to taste
- 1 can (14 oz) diced tomatoes, undrained
- 1 cup cherry tomatoes, halved
- 1/2 cup Kalamata olives, pitted and sliced
- 1/2 cup crumbled feta cheese
- Fresh parsley, chopped (for garnish)
- Cooked couscous or rice (for serving)

Instructions:

Brown the Beef:
- In a large skillet, heat olive oil over medium-high heat.
- Add lean ground beef to the skillet and cook until it is browned, breaking it apart with a spatula.

Saute Aromatics:
- Add finely chopped onion and minced garlic to the skillet. Cook until the onion is softened.

Season:
- Stir in dried oregano, dried basil, dried thyme, paprika, salt, and black pepper. Mix well to coat the beef with the spices.

Add Tomatoes:
- Pour in the can of diced tomatoes (with their juices) and add halved cherry tomatoes. Stir to combine.

Simmer:
- Allow the mixture to simmer for about 10-15 minutes, allowing the flavors to meld and the sauce to thicken slightly.

Add Olives and Feta:

- Stir in sliced Kalamata olives and crumbled feta cheese. Cook for an additional 2-3 minutes until the feta is slightly melted.

Check and Adjust Seasoning:
- Taste the Mediterranean Beef Skillet and adjust the seasoning if needed. Add more salt and pepper according to your preference.

Serve:
- Spoon the beef mixture over cooked couscous or rice.
- Garnish with chopped fresh parsley.

Enjoy:
- Enjoy this flavorful and Mediterranean-inspired Beef Skillet as a delicious and satisfying meal!

This Mediterranean Beef Skillet is a quick and flavorful one-pan dish that brings together the richness of ground beef with the vibrant flavors of tomatoes, olives, and feta cheese. Serve it over couscous or rice for a complete and delicious meal that's perfect for a busy weeknight.

www.ingramcontent.com/pod-product-compliance
Lightning Source LLC
LaVergne TN
LVHW081555060526
838201LV00054B/1903